A Letter to My Mother

"A Letter to My Mother"
Written by Cheryl Barton

Salutes to Mothers & Grandmothers
Compiled by: Cheryl Barton

Barton Publishing, LLC
P.O. Box 962
Reisterstown, Maryland 21136
www.bartonpublishingLLC.com
Phone: 443-379-3612
Email: publisher@bartonpublishingLLC.com

Ordering Information:
Quantity sales. Special discounts are available on quantity purchases by corporations, associations and others. For details contact the publisher at the address above.

ISBN:0692467416
ISBN-13: 978-0692467411

DEDICATION

This book is dedicated to my mother, Barbara Barton.
I Love you Momma!

ACKNOWLEDGEMENTS

Thank you to JoAnn Wilson, Mary J. Demory, Adrienne Melton-Better, Barbara White and my daughter Chynae Barton for your contributions to this project. I am honored to work with you as we celebrate mothers and grandmothers and the love, honor and respect we have for who they are and what they mean to us. We are because of them!

CONTRIBUTING WRITERS

A Letter to My Mother: A Short Story
By Cheryl Barton

My Mom – Mrs. Lelia Elliott
By JoAnn Wilson

My Mother Like No Other – Barbara Barton
By Cheryl Barton

Tribute to Mother Dear
By Mary J. Demory

To My "GOMMY" – Barbara Barton
By Chynae Barton

A Letter to My Mother
Shirley Ann Melton
By Adrienne Melton Better

In Dedication to My Mother Who Was My Rock and
My Foundation - Cleo Davis
By: Barbara White

The Style and Grace of My Grandmother
Mary E. Barton
By Cheryl Barton

My Mommy
By Chynae Barton

Chapter 1

"Hey Dad, are you here?" Houston hollered as she entered her parents' home. She had an hour left before her shift began at the hospital where she works as a registered nurse. She hated being late, but when her father called saying he needed to talk to her about an urgent matter, she knew nothing could keep her from coming by to see what was going on.

"He'll be right in Houston," her step-mother Anna said, coming into the room.

"Oh, hi Anna. Do you know what this urgent matter is my dad wants to talk to me about?" she asked.

Houston watched as Anna looked away, not able to look her in the eye. She knew then that Anna knew and she also knew that Anna wouldn't tell her. Whatever it was, it must be serious, she thought.

"Don't quiz your mother when I told you I would tell you when you got here," her father said entering the room.

Nicholas Ray was the greatest man Houston knew

and also the best father any girl could have. She turned at the sound of his voice, smiled and ran into his outstretched arms.

"You were sounding all mysterious on the phone and I was anxious to find out what's so important. You know how you can be all drama-like," she said making fun of the slang her younger twin sisters used.

"I'm going to finish laundry while you two talk," Anna said, in words filled with concern. Houston looked from Anna to her father and noticed he had the same worried look on his face.

"Okay, enough of this, so tell me what's going on," she said, losing patience with not knowing..

As Anna left, Houston joined her father in the sitting room, her favorite place to sit and read as a child growing up.

"Come and sit down Houston," he said, appearing nervous as he clasped his hands together in a manner that let Houston know he had something bad to tell her.

"Just say it since you know I like the bandage on a wound ripped off quickly and not slowly," she said making reference to her desire to always get bad news quick and up front and not have it dragged out.

"Your mother is in a coma in a hospital in California."

Houston was confused considering she'd just seen her mother in the next room. Perhaps her father meant to say another name.

"What are you talking about. Anna seems fine to

me."

"Not that mother Houston; I'm talking about your birth mother, Rachel. She's had some kind of accident and is in the hospital and they aren't sure she's going to make it."

Houston stood suddenly, finding it hard to breathe as she tried to wrap her thoughts around his words. She hadn't heard that name in a long time and she'd tried for years to not think about the woman who walked out on her when she was an infant. Her heart began to beat rapidly in her chest at a pace unfamiliar to her. A woman she'd never met, but that she felt close to because her blood ran through her very own veins, was dying before she'd ever been able to set eyes on her.

"Houston, are you okay? Take your time and ask me whatever you need to," she heard her father say calmly.

She paced trying to gather her thoughts, not knowing where to begin with her questions. There was much she wanted to know.

Through the years her father tried to answer questions about her mother, but she knew he was holding back, not wanting to tarnish the memory of her mother for her. He'd always told her that it wasn't his place to tell her mother's story and that he hoped one day Rachel would tell her own story to Houston, but that day never came and Houston had resolved that she would never get to meet the woman who gave her life.

She turned back to her father, not just to ask questions, but for the comfort she knew she'd find by looking into his face.

"What happened to her?" she asked coming back to sit next to him.

"I don't know all of the details other than she was in a car accident and that her injuries are pretty severe. She slipped into a coma a few days ago and they aren't offering her family much hope."

Houston's radar went up when she heard her father say the word, 'family'.

"What family? You've always said she didn't have any family?"

Houston remembered her father telling her when he'd met Rachel many years ago that she was living with a foster family and that she had no biological family that he knew of.

Her father continued on.

"The family I'm speaking of is her husband, Marcus Ealy and her son Mark."

Houston's reaction to hearing that Rachel had a son showed on her face in a way that put her father's guard up.

"Her name is Rachel Ealy and she's been alive all this time with a husband and a son?" she asked.

"Houston, before you fly off the handle, yes Rachel has a husband and son and until her accident, she was well and living in California. Her son is in his twenties and in the Navy and I knew nothing about him or her husband until yesterday. Let me try to explain as much as I can about what I know based on what I was told."

Houston knew to calm herself down and not get

angry or even feel jealous about the fact that a woman who didn't want her desired and had another child, one who got to grow up with her.

"Rachel must have known where we were, but for how long I don't know. Her best friend Lana came to see me at the office yesterday and at the time, I thought she was a new client when she asked to speak to me. I sat in my office while she explained to me who she was. I should have recognized her since she's an actress. She told me about the accident and that Rachel has been living in California for some years now after spending some time overseas with her husband who recently retired from the military. They made their home in California some years ago. She also mentioned that she was able to locate me because Rachel told her who I was and had also told her about you. She didn't go into detail about how much she knew about you, but she didn't want Rachel to pass away and you not know that she was still alive all this time."

Houston shook her head, not believing that her father was telling her that Rachel was alive all these years, obviously knew where they were and made no effort to contact them.

"I can't believe she's been alive this whole time."

"I know this comes as a shock Houston. Lana told me that the accident happened about a week ago. She's apparently in really bad shape. From what I understand, her husband has agreed to a date of when he will allow them to remove her from life support. Lana told him that she wanted to reach out to you to see if you wanted to fly out to California and then he would make the decision on the date. There is no pressure here for you to do anything and whatever you decide to do, I'm in full support of it. Houston, I know you don't know her and there were a lot of years of hurt that you and I had to work through, so you think on this and if you want to go, I'll go with you, stand with you and comfort you in any way you need. If you decide you don't want to do anything at all, I will respect and support that too."

Nicholas Ray waited, practically holding his breath waiting on his daughter to take it all in. He knew it was painful for her to hear that Rachel had been alive for the past thirty years, all of Houston's life, and had not once tried to reach out and contact them. He didn't care how long it took, he would sit and remain quiet until she let him know how he could help her through this.

"Daddy she could die and it would be life as usual for me since it's like she's been dead for the past thirty years anyway."

She looked to him for support in the way she was feeling.

"Does that sound too harsh or even morbid? I don't want it to sound that way. I don't know how to react to this. My first thought is to not go and feel the hurt all over again of her being snatched from my life as if she's walking away again. My second thought is, though she is in a coma, I would like to see her before she passes away. I don't know if I would have anything to say, but

I'd like the goodbye to be on my terms and not hers like it was thirty years ago. I want to know what you think about what I should do."

Houston grasped her father's hands and as they looked at each other for comfort, she knew that he would give her his honest opinion without judgement.

"It doesn't sound harsh or even morbid for you to feel that way. Your feelings about Rachel are yours. If for no other reason than to look upon her and have the chance to say goodbye, which is something you have been unable to do all these years, I say do it. If this is all you get of Rachel, then this will be all that you will need. God allowed Lana to reach out to me yesterday when I know that she could have let Rachel slip away and die and never tell us about it. This could be exactly what you need to finally get closure, though it's not the closure you'd want. We do have one thing that we have to consider and that is, I don't know the date that her husband will choose to have her removed from life support and your wedding is coming up in a month. I don't want this to put a damper on your special day. I've been looking forward to walking you down the aisle to give you away to Noah. This shouldn't be a cloud over that day."

Houston was set to marry the love of her life, Noah in just over thirty days. She needed to talk to Noah because her mind was made up.

"I know and I need to talk to Noah about all this since it impacts him too. There's a lot to think about and still a lot to do for the wedding."

Her father shook his head in agreement with her.

"Yes there is. I have a phone number for Lana if you would like to get the latest on Rachel's condition. I told her I would either let her know myself or have you call her with your plans. What are you thinking about doing?" he asked.

Houston thought about what he'd said and agreed that the little bit of closure she could get from this would be worth the lifetime of hurt and pain she'd always felt, not knowing why her mother never wanted her.

"I'm going to go see her to say my goodbye. I only have one more week of work before taking the next two months off for the wedding, honeymoon and moving out of my condo and into our new home. I'm going to ask if I can take the extra week and go as soon as possible after I've discussed this with Noah. I'll give Lana a call today to see if the family has made any decisions about life support. I want to get there before they do."

This wasn't the conversation she wanted to eventually have with her father about her birth mother, but she was thankful that he told her. Lana didn't have to come all this way to tell him about Rachel and he didn't have to tell her. He could have let her live her life never knowing, especially if Rachel passed away. As far as she was concerned, in her mind, Rachel had died years ago. That thought gave her comfort instead of the other option which was that Rachel was happily living a life and never thought about the daughter she left behind.

"Thank you Daddy, for loving me so much. I know hearing that Rachel has been alive all these years is as much a shock for you as it is for me. She left us thirty years ago and never looked back. I don't know why, but I'm hoping to get some peace and understanding from my visit to see her. I know you want to be there with me and for me through all of this, but I want to go alone. I have so much I want to think about and I'd like to take some time for reflection. I may stay more than one day and Anna and my sisters need you here. I promise I will call you often and anytime you want to check on me, I will have my phone on day and night. Let me talk to Lana and Noah and then I'll let you know my plans. I hope you're okay with that."

Houston wanted to tread lightly and didn't want her father's feelings hurt knowing that even after all these years and the good life and unconditional love that he and Anna have given her, that she still longed to see Rachel.

"I'm following your lead on this and I will be here in any capacity that you need. Promise me that before you board a plane going anywhere, that you will take some time and pray about forgiveness. I've told you many times in the past that even though I was hurt when she left us, I forgave her a long time ago because you can't live a life consumed with hate for someone because they didn't choose the life you wanted them to choose. Whatever Rachel's reasons were, they were her reasons and though I know you missed having a mother in your life before I married Anna, God has blessed your life tremendously. Pray for clarity and understanding and don't question why God has made the decision to call Rachel home before you can have a chance to have her as a part of your life. Know that He is responsible for granting you this little time with Rachel, so make it count. I love you and day or night, you pick up that phone if you need to hear my voice and if you need me there, I'll be on the first flight out."

Houston nodded her head as a few tears fell to her cheek. She loved her father and was thankful that he had always been there for her, never giving up on her.

"Thank you Daddy and because I've watched you live your life without regret, without hatred or anger over Rachel, I promise you I will pray about forgiveness and understanding. Thank you for showing me early in my life who God is and because of that, I know I can make it through this and will be able to walk away without any hatred in my heart. I believe I need to do this in order to finally put closure to the unknown even if it's just to see her and not hear from her."

She stood to leave and as her father stood, she hugged him with a tight bear hug. He has always put her first, took care of her and never gave her reason to doubt that he loved her more than anything. They've always had a special bond and because of that, she knew he would help see her through this.

"I love you Dad."

"I love you too, Houston. You have always been that breath of fresh air that makes everything in my life worth living. I'm proud of you and we will both make it through this. I'll tell your sisters you were here since they're still in school."

"Tell them I'll call them later. I want to know what they think of their dresses for the wedding. They had final fittings yesterday and they looked gorgeous. I'll go give Anna a hug before I leave. I know I don't have to tell her, but I want her to know how much I love her, especially with all of this with Rachel. Nothing and no one could ever take her place in my life as the mother who gives me love and support. She stepped into her role as my mother and I'm thankful for her."

Chapter 2

In California, Houston settled into her hotel room procrastinating about making the trip the few blocks to the hospital to visit the woman who gave birth to her thirty years ago and walked away. Her original plan before she boarded her flight from Florida to California was to go straight to the hospital and get that first glimpse of Rachel over and done with. She hoped doing so would alleviate the butterflies in her stomach, the nervous twitching and the lack of sleep she'd encountered since the moment her father explained to her what had happened to Rachel.

All of those plans changed the moment she landed and she realized she wasn't quite ready.

As she stood in the middle of the airport upon her arrival, waiting for her luggage to come down the conveyor belt, she had thoughts of booking another flight and returning to her comfort zone where her father, step-mother, sisters and fiancé all lived. That life she knew and she could deal with. The newness that

Rachel was alive and living in California was something she wasn't ready for.

She was in the middle of making the biggest step of her life, to walk down the aisle and marry the love of her life when the information about her birth mother rocked her world. Many thoughts ran through her mind as she thought back over the thirty years of her life that Rachel missed out on.

Houston knew that she'd had a life that she would never, ever complain about. The life her father provided for her was one filled with love and happiness and once he'd married her step-mother Anna, she'd felt the love of a mother that so many of her friends often bragged about. She loved her step-mother and no woman could ask for a better mother, but deep down, she knew that there would always be the void of where her birth mother should have been. Each time she'd met a milestone in her life, her thoughts would turn to what it would have been like if her birth mother had been in attendance. There had been thirty years of ups and downs in her life that most girls would love to be able to share their mothers. Those thoughts had her on the plane jotting down as many events over her life as she could remember. The idea occurred to her that though Rachel may not be able to hear her, she would try and recount for her something from each year of her life, write it down and share them with her. This, she knew, was more for her than for Rachel.

Before leaving for California, she'd made the decision to stay for a month. She'd gotten the all clear to add her last week of work to her vacation, so work wasn't a concern. She'd also talked to her father and Noah about her decision and neither hesitated to support her decision. This was something deep down she knew she had to do and now there was no turning back. She was now in California staying at a hotel for the next thirty days.

Houston looked at the notebook she'd brought along with her and flipped through the first few pages of notes she'd taken. She had a lot to share that Rachel had missed out on, she thought.

It was now or never as she took out her cell phone to call Marcus and Lana to let them know she had arrived.

According to her last conversation with Marcus, hospital would continue to monitor Rachel's progress for the next thirty days and if they saw no improvement, on the thirty-first day at five in the afternoon, they would be removing the life support that was keeping Rachel alive and she would be gone.

The next thirty days of Rachel in a coma was all that she would get and then she'd return to her life in Florida.

Noah understood when she asked if they could postpone their wedding for two months. She loved him and knew from the start that he was a kind and loving man. His mother agreed to work out the details for the postponement while she took care of what she needed to do in California.

She nervously dialed Marcus as she thought of what her reaction would be to seeing Rachel for the first time.

"Hello Marcus, it's Houston," she said when he answered on the first ring.

"Hello Houston. Are you here in California?"

"Yes, I landed and just checked into my hotel. I was going to get some rest before going to the hospital, but I think I want to go ahead and go now. I'm not sure how much rest I'd get until after I've seen her. Is that okay with you?"

"Absolutely, it's okay with me. How long are you staying in California? I spoke with your father a few hours ago and I promised him I'd look out for you while you were here."

Her father hadn't mentioned to Marcus that she'd be staying until life support was removed.

"Yes, about that; I'm actually going to stay until the hospital removes life support. I thought about it and I don't want to be in Florida not knowing what's going on. I don't want to intrude on your time with her and if you think that's a problem, I will follow your wishes."

"Houston, my wish is for you to deal with this in any way you feel you need to deal with this. If you want to stay for the next month, that's fine with me. I do have one request if you plan to stay that long."

"Yes?" she asked.

"There is plenty of room here at the house and rather than stay at a hotel, I'd like for you to think about staying here at the house. My housekeeper, Ms. Sophia is here all day every day and she loves taking care of us. I think you'd be more comfortable here than at a hotel for thirty days, so think about it, talk to your father and let me know. I was about to head over to the hospital in a few minutes so I'll come by and pick you up so you won't have to catch a cab. There is also an extra car around here that you can use while you are here. I know this is a strange situation, but I feel it's my duty to look after you while you're here. I know Rachel would want me to and as a father, I know your father would feel better knowing you're being looked after and not alone in a hotel."

"Thank you Marcus, that's very nice of you and I would appreciate a ride to the hospital. I'll let you know about everything else later today if that's okay. I can't seem to think of anything else right now other than Rachel and seeing her."

"That's sounds great. I'm on my way to get you. Give me the name of the hotel and I'll give you a call when I get there."

**

Houston walked into Rachel's hospital room and held her breath as she peered down at the woman who gave her life. The first thing she noticed was that everyone was correct in saying that she looked just like Rachel. Houston could look at her and see what she herself would look like at that age.

Walking on shaky legs, she moved even closer to the bed that sat in the center of the room. Machines beeped and tubes and wires ran from poles to Rachel's hands, face and head. Even in this state, Houston could tell that Rachel was a beautiful woman.

"Amazing isn't it?" Marcus said behind her.

"What's amazing?" she asked.

"How much you look like her. The resemblance is incredible."

"Yes, I do see what you, my dad and Lana have been saying. My dad always told me I look just her."

"I'm going to go check in with her doctor and I'll give you some privacy."

"Okay, thank you Marcus," she said watching him as he first walked over and kissed Rachel on the cheek before turning to head back out of the room.

She was now alone with Rachel and wasn't sure what to do. Her legs were shaking and before she fell to the floor, she grabbed a chair, pulled it up to the bed and sat down, never taking her eyes off of Rachel.

"Hi Rachel," she said nervously. "I know you don't know me, but I'm Houston. I've come a long way to see you and now that I'm here, I know this was the right decision. I don't really know what to say, but I wanted to let you know that I was here and that I turned out okay. I don't know what you've thought about me all these years, but Dad did a great job of raising me pretty much on his own. I'm sorry this happened to you and I hope you're not feeling any pain. I'll be here for the next thirty days and I plan to visit you every day."

Though it felt as if she were talking to herself, it felt therapeutic that she could talk so freely.

"On the plane ride here to California, I thought about how I could make these thirty days with you count. This is not the typical situation for a visit with someone, but I want to be sure that I don't waste this time that God is allowing us to have even if you can't hear me. What I've decided to do is for the next thirty days, I'm going to share something from the thirty years of my life. I'm going to pick something that I can remember from each year and share it with you and if there is a chance you can hear me, I'm hoping you can take these words to heaven with you, feeling no regret about leaving me all those years ago. For today, I'll start with year one of my life, the year you left.

Chapter 3
Day 1, Age 1

"My dad told me that you left right before my first birthday so you wouldn't know this and I don't remember it, but I've seen pictures that show me in a pink and white frilly dress that he thought I looked cute in. I think that frilly dress is what started me on the path of being particular about how I look. I still love to dress up when I'm going out and I'm what you would still call a girly-girl, though that wasn't always the case, it's definitely who I am now.

There were lots of kids at the party and even a clown and my dad says I was terrified of him so he only lasted a few short minutes before he left because I wouldn't stop crying. At thirty, I'm still terrified of clowns. I have no idea why.

Daddy stuck to what he called tradition and he had two cakes for my birthday party. One was for everyone else and the other was for me to play in and from the pictures, it looks like I really dug in. There was cake everywhere; all in my hair, all over my clothes, the floor and even all over my dad because when he tried to pick me up, I smeared cake all over his face and hair.

We lived with grandma and grandpa because my dad was still in college and he needed them to help look after me.

My best friend, Ivory, was at my party that day. We have been best friends for thirty years. She is also going to serve as the maid of honor at my wedding. I'll tell you more about wedding stuff later.

Daddy said that Ivory and I were inseparable the day of my party. We rode ponies together and walked around hand in hand the whole party. Ivory and her family lived right next door to us. I look at pictures now from that day and I realize Ivory was in every single picture that was taken of me except for a couple with my dad. I didn't know what a best friend was back then, but after all these years, we've remained closer than sisters.

Dad says that you would remember Ivory's family because for the short time that you lived at the house when you were pregnant and after you had me, they were the neighbors back then and Ivory's family was well known in the community.

I've looked at a lot of the pictures from that day and though I was happy and having a good time, I could see in some of the pictures that my dad was sad that day. I'm assuming that he was sad because you weren't there. He had hopes back then that you would come back, but as time went on, he knew that he could forget about that hope. Everyone made the best of the day and made sure it was a lot of fun despite the fact that your absence was noticeable and my dad had a hard time dealing with it. The bottom line was he made it a great day for me despite the fact that you made me a motherless child. That year, the hurt of the impact of your absence was only felt by my dad, but that wasn't always the case. I went through a few years of asking where you were. This year was a happy one and from the pictures I've seen, one filled with lots of love.

Chapter 4
Day 2, Age 2

"Hi Rachel. I'm here early today. Marcus invited me to stay at your house while I'm here and early this morning, he showed up at the hotel to help me check out and to gather me and my stuff to take me to your house.

Your husband is a wonderful person and I can see how much he loves you. He has told family and friends that no one is to visit you between eleven in the morning until one o'clock in the afternoon every day, setting this time aside for me to spend with you.

He's also loaning me a car to use while I'm here. He explained to me that the car belongs to Mark and since he's away in the Navy, it's okay for me to use it. I was a little hesitant at first thinking that Mark wouldn't want some strange person driving his car without him knowing it. He assured me Mark would be okay with it and I do enjoy the thought of being able to drive here to see you each day and to also be able to take some time to explore California and not tie up his time or Lana's time while I'm here. He wouldn't hear of me renting a car for thirty days when there is a car that I can drive without that extra added expense. Your family and friends have been very nice to me.

Your house is beautiful and so spacious. My favorite feature of your house is the swimming pool. Let me tell you how much I love to swim.

When I was two years old, my dad signed me up for swimming lessons. A little boy in our neighborhood was found unconscious in the swimming pool in his family's backyard and my dad wanted to be sure that if I was ever around a swimming pool, I would know how to swim and tread water.

My first swimming lesson didn't go well, from what I was told. Daddy took lots of pictures of me trying to claw my way over the swimming teacher's back to get out of the water. I saw one picture where I was crying and screaming to get out, but he wasn't swayed by my tears. It was more important to him that I learn how to tread water.

I was told that after three lessons, I took to the water like a fish. I not only began to love the water, but I learned how to rollover in the water in case I was in danger and I learned how to swim in three feet of water.

That was the same year that grandpa had a swimming pool built at our house and I looked forward to getting in the water every day.

After learning early how to swim, I spent a lot of years on swim teams and I won lots of swimming matches. Today, I still have all of my medals from the competitions. I told Noah that once our house was complete, the next thing I wanted to do was build a pool out back so that one day when we have our children, they'll also learn how to swim. I want to be sure I teach my children everything about safety. I look forward to being a mother and it saddens me to know that something about being a mother frightened you enough to cause you to walk away from it. I don't know how hard leaving was for you and I guess I will never know."

Chapter 5
Day 3, Age 3

"Hi Rachel. I was up late writing last night, trying to remember some things my dad told me about my year as a three year old. He claims I had a delayed reaction to being a terrible two year old and at three, I let loose with temper tantrums, crying for no reason and I had a knack for picking up and throwing things on the floor.

I was quite feisty for a three year old and according to family, I gave them all lots of attitude whenever I was told to do something I didn't want to do, like sit down or eat my food. Dad kept a picture of me from back then from one night when I wouldn't eat my food because I wanted a cupcake before dinner. He said I pouted, cried, screamed and even threw food on the floor, so he put me in my high chair and made me sit there until I ate my food. After months of dealing with my bad behavior, I think he'd finally had enough. He told me I whined and cried for him to let me down and to pick me up, but he wouldn't give in. Each time I threw my food on the floor, he would fix me a new plate of food and sat there with me until finally I gave in and ate either out of hunger or out of frustration that I wasn't getting my way. I never did get my cupcake even after I ate my food because he wasn't happy with my behavior.

To say I was stubborn is an understatement. Dad tells me now that my stubbornness definitely came from you. He told me of some of the times when you would be out together and how you were set in your ways and he always had to be the one to give in if he wanted to keep the peace. When I tried that at three, he wasn't having it and he straightened that stubborn spirit up quickly. That, I am told, is when I learned the hard lesson that there is no reward for bad behavior. I continued through my late terrible twos at the age of three, but it got better because dad said, I was a smart little girl and I realized I wasn't in control of anything at that age. I'll remember that one day when Noah and I have children. They will not be running my house!"

Chapter 6
Day 4, Age 4

"Good morning Rachel. It's me Houston and I bought you something today."

Houston reached into the big oversized bag she'd bought with her and pulled out a fleece throw.

"I went to the store yesterday after I left the hospital because I needed to pick up a few things. I'm going to be here for thirty days and I didn't bring thirty days' worth of clothes and toiletries, so I figured I would take the time and do that. I had been talking to Ms. Sophia who has already been taking great care of me. I keep asking her to let me help her or that I can do my own laundry, but she insists that she loves what she does. She's told me that she misses you and that you have always been wonderful to her.

While we were talking she mentioned to me that you love the color yellow in any shade. I saw this golden yellow throw blanket at the store with pictures of flowers on a hill on it and I thought it would look nice in your room. I've been here a few days and each day it seems to be rather chilly in here. For those days when the air may get a little extra brisk, I thought this would be nice and warm. I checked with the nurse on duty and she said that laying this across you would be fine so here it is."

Houston laid the blanket across Rachel and straightened it before sitting in her usual seat, in the chair right at the side of the bed.

"I always thought that it's nice to have one special blanket that would make a room brighter and would also brighten the spirit like something warm and cozy should do. When I was four years old, I had this blanket that was pink, white and yellow. It was my favorite and I took that blanket everywhere I went. I started pre-kindergarten this year and school or not, I wasn't going anywhere without my blanket. Daddy tried every bribe he could think of to get me to let go of the blanket the first day of school, but I wasn't having it. He tried to convince me that four year olds did not still have "blankies" anymore because I was supposed to be a big girl. I didn't care and again that stubborn streak came out and I dragged that blanket with me to school. I learned a lesson that day; if you don't want to be called a baby by a bunch of four year olds, don't act like one. When my dad picked me up later that day, he didn't see the blanket. When he asked me for it I told him I was a big girl and big girls don't carry blankets to school. My teacher had placed the blanket in a bag with a note and though I kept that blanket at home, it never made another appearance at school. What topped off my day was when my dad said, "that's my big girl."

Chapter 7
Day 5, Age 5

"Hi Rachel. It's a hot day outside today. I thought Florida was hot, but it's nothing compared to the heat of California. I went swimming in the pool at your house before coming to visit you today and it was exactly what I needed.

I talked to Daddy and Noah early this morning to let them know that I was doing well and that my daily visits to you are the highlight of my day. I feel like a weight is being lifted when I come here and share my life with you.

I was exhausted when I got in last night so I went to lie down and when I woke up, it was morning. Marcus said my dad had called him because he couldn't reach me and he was worried. Marcus offered to wake me, but my dad said to let me sleep. I had been out all day, spending most of it at the hospital and then last night with Lana who invited me over for dinner. We kept the evening light and per my wishes, I didn't want her to tell me things about you that you couldn't tell me yourself, so we talked about Lana's career as an actress. You sure do know some famous people Rachel."

Houston smiled as she leaned over and moved some hair that was lying across Rachel's face.

"I guess when they bathed you this morning, they forgot to comb your hair. I'll see if they can give me a comb and straighten it for you."

The nurse gladly gave Houston a comb and careful not to disturb any of the wires, she combed Rachel's hair making sure not one strand was out of place.

"You know we would look like twins if I hand blond streaks in my hair like yours. It's a nice look for you. Now that you're all dolled up, let me tell you about the time I had my first fight at age five because a boy pulled my hair. Even at that age, one should never, ever touch a girl's hair without asking first," she laughed.

Houston reached for her phone to be sure it was on in case her father called again and this time she sat it on the table in front of her.

"When I was five years old, there was this very mean boy named Bobby in my class. Every day he would find some reason to pick on me. He would pull on my shirt or try to take a snack from my lunch box. One day, he pulled on my ponytail. My hair is shorter now, but back then I hand ponytails that came all the way down my back. He wanted to know why I had to have barrettes in my hair every day saying they were ugly. He must have pulled my hair about ten times that day and I warned him to stop. He said I wasn't going to do anything because I was a girl. I should have told him that my dad taught me how to protect myself and that I wasn't scared of any boys.

When we went to the playground, I was about to get on the swing when he ran up and pulled my ponytail really hard to the point that it actually hurt. Before he knew what was happening, I balled my fist up and hit him right in the face. I remember doing that and when he didn't move, I hit him again. Then I kept hitting him and punching him until a teacher came and broke it up. When my dad picked me up from school, he was told that I punched on a boy. He promised the school he would take care of it and he apologized for me. I didn't want him to apologize because Bobby had it coming.

When I got home, my dad asked me what happened and I told him Bobby kept pulling on my hair. He asked me if I hit him with the right hook he showed me and I said yes. He said, 'way to go champ and the next time he touches you, try the left hook too.' That's my Daddy!

Bobby never touched my hair again and after that day, he would tell all the kids that I was his girlfriend. I guess I had my first boyfriend at five years old because I punched him in the face."

Chapter 8
Day 6, Age 6

"Good morning Rachel and it's a rainy day in California today, something I knew even before I heard the rain."

Houston looked down and rubbed her aching wrist, a slight pain she experienced every time it rained.

"I sat up writing my daily passage to you and out of nowhere my wrist started aching and I immediately declared that it was going to rain."

Houston sat down and pulled out her notebook to read what she'd written the night before.

"Let me tell you about how my wrist became the weather predictor. When I was six, I would watch a cartoon and the little girl had a tree house that was pink and white and it had a ladder that led up to the door and inside was enough room for a table with chairs and a place to put toys and books. After seeing that, I begged my dad for a treehouse and I wanted him to build it in the great big tree in grandpa's back yard.

Of course he said no, but that didn't stop me from begging him for it every chance I got.

One day I wanted to see how far I would be able to see if I had a tree house in the tree and maybe dad would then build me one. I climbed the tree, even though I knew I shouldn't and though it was easy to climb up, it wasn't as easy to climb down and before I knew it, I fell out of the tree and broke my wrist. I can remember seeing dad running out of the house to get to me with a fear of death on his face. I think he was more terrified than me.

I never did get my tree house, but I did get a pretty pink cast that all of my family and friends signed and a permanent warning sign of bad weather. Later that year, I did get a pretty pink and white doll house and dad said he wanted me to stay out of trees, not just for my safety, but for his health. He has always been a worrier and thankfully, my protector as well because that's what parents are supposed to be to their children. You should know, that even though I don't understand why you left me, my dad did a great job of looking after me.

Chapter 9
Day 7, Age 7

"Hi Rachel. I've been here for a whole week and I have to say I love California. Noah told me not to get any thoughts about life on the west coast because he is expecting me back home in Florida."

Houston got comfortable and began her visit.

"Last night I went to the set of Lana's latest television series. I had a great time and she introduced me to a lot of the stars that I had only seen on television and I felt like a kid in a candy store. I was, as they say, star-struck. She told me I can come back for any of the tapings while I'm still here in California and I'm planning on going back tonight. Let me go get me a bottle of water before I tell you about my own experience with acting. You have missed many years of my starring roles."

Houston straighten Rachel's blanket to be sure she was staying warm and went in search of the water. When she returned, she took her seat and the words, like all of the other days, flowed easily from the pages of her book.

"When I was seven I took part in my first play. Daddy was quite adamant that I had to stay involved in extra activities to keep me busy. He didn't like idle time unless I was reading which is something else I love doing.

This particular year, my school was getting ready for the annual Christmas play and one of the teachers who also went to the same church we attended remembered hearing me sing on the children's choir and told me that I should be in the play. I asked my dad if I could since there would be rehearsals after school and he said yes and he would work his schedule so that I could attend every rehearsal. He came to most of them or some days grandpa would pick me up and sit in on the rehearsals. Since I went to a Christian school our play was about the birth of Jesus. When they heard me sing, I was asked to play the role of Mary and it came with a singing part. I wasn't nervous and on the night of the play, daddy, grandma and grandpa all came and so did other family members and most of our neighbors. They were the definition of my village.

I realized I liked acting and that carried over into high school when in my junior year, I won the part of Dorothy in our version of the Wiz, you know the one that starred Diana Ross.

After the Christmas play was over, dad gave me a dozen roses, my first time getting flowers and he took me out for ice cream. Did I mention my favorite ice cream is strawberry? To this day, any time I stop at Daddy and Anna's house, there is always a pint of strawberry ice cream in the freezer. I know it's for me because no one else, not even my sisters, Kasey and Ariel like that flavor. I wish I knew what your favorite kind of ice cream was. I wonder if we have that in common. Maybe I'll ask Mark when I have a chance to talk to him. The Navy is still trying to work out getting him home soon so that he can see you. I can't wait to meet him and maybe find out about more of your favorite things."

Chapter 10
Day 8, Age 8

"This was the year of the bicycle accident and I still have the scars to show for it. Daddy always said that I had a determined spirit because when I set my mind to something, there is no stopping me. I believe that's a good thing, but when I was eight years old, it wasn't so good.

I was a pretty good daredevil back then and the competitive nature of my personality got me in a lot of trouble. Some of the boys in my neighborhood were racing their bikes and had constructed this ramp with a board propped up on cinder blocks. I hated that they would tease me saying I road my bike like a girl. It shouldn't have bothered me considering I was a girl, but I didn't like being taunted. Daddy always told me to be careful when riding my bike and most times I was, but not on this particular day.

The boys challenged me to ride my bike over the ramp after I told them I could ride faster and better than any of them could. I didn't hesitate to take the challenge and after I was sure daddy was busy in the house, I took off on my bike as fast as I could and raced over the ramp, up into the air and flew off my bike and hit the ground hard. I was happy that I didn't break anything, but I did get some pretty deep scars especially the one on my knee.

After I hit the ground and the bike fell on me, those boys took off on their bikes as if they were never even there. A neighbor came running out to help me and that's when I saw daddy running with that look he always had when I fell or would hurt myself. He has that look that says first he wants to be sure I'm alright and then worry turns to anger when he realizes I again did not listen to him when he said to be careful. From that day forward, he called me his little daredevil and just like always, the next day I was back up on my bike and still accepting challenges. I guess I'm just tough that way."

Chapter 11
Day 9, Age 9

"Hi Rachel, I'm running a little bit late today. I went to the set of Lana's television show again last night to see the filming of the season finale and it was really good. After the show I went with Lana to a cast party to celebrate with everyone. I got to bed extremely late, but I made sure to recall what I wanted to tell you about today. I met more famous people last night and one actor tried to hit on me," Houston laughed while sitting on the edge of Rachel's bed.

"Can you believe that this big engagement ring that I'm wearing didn't deter him one bit? I told Noah about it this morning and he was ready to take the first flight out from Florida; he was joking of course. I told him he has nothing to worry about because there is no other man for me but him and no amount of fame or fortune could change that. I believe in love and commitment, something I learned from daddy at an early age."

"Houston, do you mind if I interrupt for a minute to take her vitals?" the nurse on duty asked.

"Not at all," she responded. The nurses and doctors who cared for Rachel now knew her by name since she was there every day. She didn't know why, but it brought her comfort. When the nurse was done, she pulled out her notebook and began reading.

"When I was nine years old Daddy met Anna early in the year. They had been dating a few months when one day he told me he wanted me to meet a woman he liked a lot. I knew that meant daddy had a girlfriend and I didn't care how much he liked her, I was determined I wasn't going to like her. I liked that I had him all to myself and I didn't want anyone butting in on our life.

He told me he'd made plans for us to go out to dinner and this lady was going to come along with us. We dressed up in our finest and because daddy seemed so happy, I tried to keep a smile on my face. The first thing that happened that spoiled my plan to not like her was when we picked her up, she gave me a pink gift bag with a present in it just for me. Daddy had told her how much I love dolls and she'd bought me a Barbie that had several changes of clothes in the bag. I could have done cartwheels I was so happy. Throughout dinner, Anna made sure to include me in every conversation they had. It turned out to be a fun night and at the end of the year, Anna and daddy got married and we became a family. That turned out to be one of the happiest days of my life because I really did like Anna and daddy was over the moon with happiness he was so in love.

My dad is a good guy and he always has been. Did you think he wasn't good enough for you when you walked away?"

Houston looked up from reading and looked into Rachel's face. She didn't mean for the words to come out harsh, but she also wanted to be honest with her thoughts.

"My dad would give his everything for anyone and he loves to see others happy. Why weren't you happy with him? With us? I would like to know what kind of happiness was around the corner for you that would make you never want to look back. I believe that if no one else loves a child, a mother should. I won't say that you didn't love me; I will say that now I'll never know one way or the other."

Chapter 12
Day 10, Age 10

"I wish you could see the rows and rows of trophies I have at home. I think the year that I got the most was when I was ten years old.

That year I was involved in everything including my first time playing lacrosse. For years people saw lacrosse as a sport for boys, but I was really good at it. I didn't have a sport or activity that year that I didn't excel at. I won lots of swimming medals that year and one coach tried to talk my dad into letting me compete nationally. He talked to me about it and as much as I loved swimming, I also loved softball, I took karate, I played volleyball and a few others along with dance classes and acting classes. I didn't want to give up all of those things to focus only on swimming. My dad left the decision up to me and I'm glad he did because I loved them all.

Daddy and Anna never missed a competition and were always cheering me on louder than any other parents. That year I finally knew what it felt like to have a mom around and Anna filled in right nicely being the mother that I needed and deserved. I deserved that you know. Every little girl growing up deserves to have a mother who loves and cares for her and would do anything to make her little girl smile. Anna slipped into that role and never gave it a second thought. We never talked about the fact that she wasn't the woman who gave birth to me, but she was the best mother any girl could ever have. I think back on all the fun things Anna and I didn't together and I realize you sure did miss out on a lot. I'm glad Mark had you his whole life because a mother's love is like no other when it comes to a child. I'm glad you had me and I'm even happier that Anna stepped in and provided what I needed most back then, which was someone to call mom."

Chapter 13
Day 11, Age 11

"Hi Rachel. I know you can't see me, but today I didn't put much energy into hair, makeup and attire. I woke up and just didn't feel like it. I realized yesterday how tired I was when I got back to your house and decided that it was okay to have a day that didn't take me all morning to get out in it.

I went through a stage when I was eleven where I was tired of being all girly girl. I wanted to wear jeans and sneakers all the time and I was tired of cute, frilly dresses that most little girls loved. I wanted to play basketball and was jealous of the boys who got to play football. My dad hated this phase I went through, but like a trooper Anna handled it well. Even though she didn't have any children of her own at this point, she knew how to handle being a mother. There were times when daddy wanted to force me into a dress and Anna told him to let me go through this phase, something a lot of little girls went through. This was the year that daddy started backing off and trusting Anna to do what mothers do and he took a back seat. I may have gone through this phase for a few months if it had not been for the day Anna decided to enroll me in a charm school for little girls.

I didn't know at the time that she did it to bring back the girly nature that I was trying to shun. All I knew was that I got the chance to model for local store fashion shows and catalogues and I got to keep all of the clothes I modeled. Soon my closet overflowed with more clothes that I had ever had and they were all bright and cute and I loved showing off for my friends. At that age kids thrived on the jealous nature of their friends and I was no different. Anna and I began having nights of doing each other's hair and painting or nails and in no time at all, the tomboy phase was over and a little lady was blossoming once again and I never knew that was Anna's game plan all along."

Chapter 14
Day 12, Age 12

"I started getting boobs this year. I can't begin to tell you the horror of being stirred at by boys back then.

The previous year I could pal around with them, play sports, go to the arcade and just hang out. When my boobs started to make an appearance, they started treating me differently and the looks I got let me know that I was no longer just one of the guys. I knew right then and there that those days were coming to an end.

Many of my friends were going through what I was going through, but the difference was I didn't have you around to talk about the changes in my body and to go bra shopping. Anna did all that, but it wasn't the same because it was just one more reminder that you weren't around. Anna was also pregnant this year with my sisters so she tried her best to give me as much attention as she could, but carrying two babies was hard on her and she was tired a lot. A few times I tried to talk to daddy about what I was going through and he directed me to grandma or Anna for girl talk. He was such a chicken back then.

Anna ended up taking me shopping for my very first bra and it wasn't anything special. All I can remember is that it was white and boy did the kids know that I had one on. I had a few friends who were much more developed than I was, so the bras they wore were a little more fancy and mine was more like a sports bra or what they back then called a training bra. I guess that means it was a bra to help train my boobs or something.

Until they really started coming in later in the next year, I would try to hide the imprint of the bra by wearing sweaters all the time. I don't know why that year ended up being such an embarrassment, but it was. Nothing against Anna, but I wonder if you would have helped me get through it a little easier. I guess we'll never know."

Chapter 15
Day 13, Age 13

"This was the best and the worst year for me. Womanhood claimed me this year and even though Anna tried to prepare me for what was to come, I still wanted you. I wanted you to be there to celebrate woman's day with me, to take me out shopping, to go for ice cream and to hear from you all of the things I should watch out for when it came to boys. Daddy cowered away from any discussions about womanhood, not wanting to believe I was finally crossing over. He wanted me to stay his little girl forever.

I didn't tell Anna or Daddy, but every night I prayed that God would send you home to me so that I could be like all of my other friends whose mom's took them out for a special celebration. They would enjoy many mother and daughter outings and though I appreciated Anna's attempt to fill the void that you left, I still longed for the mother that gave me life, the woman where if I looked in her face, I saw some of myself. I wanted to know who you were, what you looked like, what kind of life you were living that you didn't want to include me in. More than ever, this year I wanted answers and they just didn't come.

Daddy and I had many conversations about you, but the most important questions, he wouldn't answer. I would ask why you left and Daddy would say he couldn't answer that for you because if he did, his response would be one-sided, from his perspective and it was a story that only you could tell. I would ask him where you lived and if you were still alive and he would say, he didn't know. I asked him if you had family that I could meet and he said he had never met your family. I longed for you so many nights and the images of you wouldn't come and the memories were not there. I was left with nothing and that nothingness haunted me because I didn't know if I was the blame for your absence. My dad assured me I wasn't, but he also couldn't provide me with the answer to why. More of what I now know will never come."

Chapter 16
Day 14, Age 14

"Now fourteen was a good year because I entered high school and everything changed. I continued with cheerleading and I also played volleyball, had small roles in some of the school plays and of course I joined the dance team. This was the first year of the best four years of my life.

I had no idea I would like high school so much and let me tell you, the boys really began to notice me. I went from barely having any boobs to having them larger than most of my teachers. Puberty hit hard and fast and though it made me popular in school because I really blossomed, Anna sat me down and we talked about life, boys and sex and that I needed to stay clear away from the latter until I was married. That's what all parents say and at that time, I was so busy with activities, the last thing I was concerned about was boys. I flirted with them, but that was as far as it went for me.

I excelled athletically and academically and my dad and Anna where happy about that because they could see that I wasn't boy crazy like some of my other friends. I did have lots of questions about boys and sex and when I first asked my dad a few, you would have thought I'd asked him about committing a crime. He stuttered over his words and began sweating like he was running a marathon. He wasn't expecting me to hit him with a ton of questions when he asked me how my day was going. He told me to give him a minute and I looked up and he'd sent Anna in his place. I laughed realizing this was not a father, daughter conversation. Thank goodness Anna jumped right in and handled my questions like only a mother could do.

It was moments like these that made me realize how much you've missed out on. My life could have been filled with unanswered questions if it had not been for her. The nitty-gritty of the sex talk for a girl is something she expects to have with her mother and if my dad had not married, who knows who I would have gotten the details from. I know I wouldn't want it from any of my friends because within a year, a few of them were already pregnant. I guess the talk didn't go so well for them.

There are stages in a girl's life where she needs her mother and times like when I wanted to know all about sex, I wondered about you the most. I had Anna and I was thankful for that, but still, she wasn't you and you should have been there. You just should have been there."

Chapter 17
Day 15, Age 15

"Hi Rachel. I fell asleep early last night so I had to get up early this morning to write down what I wanted to share with you. I stayed up most of the night talking to Noah on the phone. I've missed him so much being away from him for the past two weeks. He's going to fly in for the weekend to visit me and to check on me in person. I started to tell him he didn't have to do that because he was already sacrificing so much for me, but I want to see him; I need to see him in order to get a touch of reality from back home.

I bought some gowns for you today. I told Marcus that I thought that it would be nice to get you out of these ugly hospital gowns for a change and he agreed. I hear the nurse coming to get you changed so I'm going to step out to grab a bite to eat, but I'll be back when they're done."

Houston stepped out just as the nurses were coming in. She told them she'd return shortly and thanked them for re-dressing Rachel when she knew they didn't have to.

"You look beautiful Rachel," Houston said when she returned to find Rachel dressed in a beautiful red gown and knew the suggestion was the right one.

"Let's get to the year I turned fifteen and went to my first school dance. We had a sophomore dance and as soon as the school announced we were having it, a few boys asked me to go and I said yes to one boy in particular and his name was Keith. We not only had classes together at school, he also lived in the same neighborhood.

This was an exciting time and instead of Anna taking me shopping for a dress to wear, daddy turned it into a fun day with just he and I. The twins were at an age where they kept Anna and daddy busy all the time and so whenever he thought I may not be getting the attention I should be getting, he would take the time and let me pick a day of fun things just for him and me to do. That day we had lunch at my favorite pizza place and then we went to the mall and found the perfect dress.

The day of the dance, as soon as I got out of school, Anna took me to the hair salon and I got my long and very thick hair blown out and this was also the first time that I was allowed to get designs on my fingers and toe nails. Anna and my dad were very old fashioned, but today I appreciate the things they didn't allow me to do because others were doing them. Anna said it was time, though daddy tried to fight it saying he wanted to keep me as his little girl as long as possible.

It was too late for that because didn't he realize I was fifteen and back then I thought I was already a woman.

I wish you could have seen me back then all spruced up and heading to my first dance. Daddy drove me and Keith to the dance and Keith's dad was responsible for picking us up and dropping me at home. I was nervous for most of the night because all of my friends kept telling me that Keith would try to kiss me when his dad dropped me off. I had never been kissed by a boy before and so the entire night I couldn't think of anything else other than what I would do if he tried to kiss me. At the end of the night, I had nothing to worry about. Keith shook my hand and told me he had a fun time and thanked me for being his date. I'm sure his father probably told him not to try anything.

You've missed so many fun and exciting times in my life Rachel. It feels good to relive my life in order to share it with you, but I want you to know that my preference would have been to have you there for each and every year to experience it like a mother should."

Chapter 18
Day 16, Age 16

"This was a busy year. Daddy had a business trip to Paris and since the trip was in the summer, he took me with him and I had a great time touring the country. I think it was because I met a boy I wanted to date and my dad thought I wasn't ready for a serious boyfriend yet, so he heaved a sigh of relief when he realized he could take me away for six weeks and he wouldn't have to worry about it just yet.

Anna stayed home with the twins while daddy and I took the trip and I'd never seen a more beautiful place. We stayed in a magnificent hotel and after he finished up his work for the day, we spent hours touring Paris.

I never told him this, but I met a boy in Paris that summer and that was where I had my very first kiss. It wasn't one of those little pecks on the cheek or a quick kiss on the lips either. It was how I first learned how to French kiss and it was sloppy, but nice. We exchanged addresses and phone numbers before daddy and I headed back home, but we didn't stay in touch. I couldn't wait to get back to tell all of my girlfriends about my French boyfriend for six weeks and how he taught me to French kiss. Imagine my surprise when I realized I was the last in my group to experience a French kiss. It wasn't as exciting to them as I thought it would be, but it was a summer I'll never forget.

I hear that you spent some time in Paris before. I wonder if it were possible that we could have crossed paths in Paris and never knew it. Wouldn't that have been something? Travel to another country and run into someone who looks just like you."

Chapter 19
Day 17, Age 17

Houston entered Rachel's room and stopped in her tracks. She looked to where the bed should be and the spot was empty. She stepped back out to be sure she had entered the right room and as she read the room number over and over, she realized she had the right room, but Rachel wasn't in it.

A fear like nothing she'd ever experienced came over her as she thought of what Rachel's absence could mean. She looked around as hospital staff went about their jobs and no one seemed to notice her presence though they've seen her every day for the past two weeks. If anything had happened, she knew they would call Marcus and someone would have said something to her by now, so she calmed her nerves and walked toward one of the nurses.

"Excuse me, do you know where Rachel Ealy is? I noticed she's not in her room."

"Yes, she was taken down for some tests. She should be back up in a few minutes if you want to wait in her room."

Houston exhaled and immediately felt better.

"Thank you."

She turned back around and took her usual seat in Rachel's room and waited.

She didn't have to wait long when she turned toward a sound and noticed orderlies rolling Rachel back into the room and situating her back in the space Houston was use to her being in. After Rachel was once again made comfortable and all of the machines keeping her alive where checked, she was once again alone with her and pulled out her notebook to read through what she wrote about being seventeen.

"I got my driver's license this year and between daddy's car and Anna's car, I always had a car to drive. Anna didn't work outside the house so most days I used her car. This was the first year I really felt free. Daddy was overprotective like a father should be and Anna always worried about me driving on the road, but there were days when I'd get in the car and drive around with no particular destination in mind. Let me tell you how hard it was to get my license. I passed the test for my permit with no problem, but when it came to parking and this three point turn for the test, I failed three times. One day my grandpa said that I was going to pass on the next time around and he would see to it.

He took me driving in one of the school parking lots and each day, he would instruct me on the turn and the parking until I had perfected it. When it came time for the test, he took me and when you failed the test, the instructor would be driving the car back to the front of the building. This time, I saw grandpa almost leap in the air when I was driving when we pulled back up to the front of the building. That was a proud moment that I'll never forget. Milestones are major stepping stones in a child's life that should never be missed. Not only did you miss everything, but now you're going miss all of the new ones too."

Chapter 20
Day 18, Age 18

"This was the year of all years because this was high school graduation. A lot occurred this year leading up to graduation.

There was prom to get ready for and since I had a steady boyfriend, I also went to his senior prom which was for another school. We met at the mall one day and it turns out he went to the school that was the biggest rival against my school. We hit it off when we first met and from day one, we were inseparable. We did a lot of fun things and spent a lot of time together under my dad's watchful eye of course. It was fun having a boyfriend and he was someone daddy actually liked. Believe me, daddy wouldn't like him if he ever knew how many times that same boyfriend tried to talk me into drinking and other activities I won't even mention right now. Let's just say I was listening every time daddy told me the reasons why I needed to avoid temptation and I'm glad I did.

After graduation I got the biggest surprise of my life when daddy bought me my very own car. I spent that summer before college just hanging out and having fun. I was going to get a part time job, but daddy told me that he was so proud of my accomplishments in school that he wanted me to have fun for the summer before going away to college.

I was heartbroken when my boyfriend and I went away to different colleges quite a distance from each other. I ended up going to college in Virginia and he went to college in Texas. By this time we were now living in Florida. We tried to stay in touch and keep the relationship going, but the distance was against us and eventually we broke up.

I went to college to be a nurse and it wasn't until after I graduated that daddy told me that during the time when the two of you were together, you'd mentioned that you always wanted to be a nurse. I realized I was a lot like you and didn't even know you. I bet we have even more in common than either of us know or will ever know now."

Chapter 21
Day 19, Age 19

"I lost my virginity at nineteen and wished I could get it back because he wasn't worth the effort and the couple of seconds he lasted. It was nothing like I'd heard from other girls and read about in those romance novels we were all reading. While I tried to get use to the immediate pain, it was already over and it turned out that he was more embarrassed than I was. For the rest of the semester, he said nothing else to me. If he saw me, he would go the opposite direction.

When I went home on break from school, I cried in Anna's lap and she told me everything would be alright. She always said she hoped I would wait until I was really ready for the emotional responsibility that came along with intimacy because if it didn't turn out well, she knew there would be hurt and pain and how he treated me was a hard pill to swallow.

I ran into him a few more times that year and the following year and then one day he was gone from school. I heard he'd gotten a girl on campus pregnant and he had to leave school to get a job. I'm glad that wasn't me and I really dodged a bullet. The one thing I never wanted was to have children at that age and definitely not without being married.

You must have been really scared when you were pregnant with me at such a young age and didn't know what you were going to do. I remember clearly being nineteen and I had a hard enough time deciding what outfit to wear each day. I can't imagine having to make a big life decision like having a baby the way you did.

Now that I'm older, I try to understand the decision you made to walk away. I've often asked daddy why and he always tells me the same thing, which is, he doesn't know. He always said that he hoped wherever you were that you were happy because he knew it couldn't have been easy for you to make the choice to leave me. I hope your life has been a happy one Rachel."

Chapter 22
Day 20, Age 20

"College life had turned around for me by the time I turned twenty. I finally decided to put the hurt and disappointment of the year before behind me and I moved on.

One day as I was walking across campus a friend from one of my classes gave me an envelope inviting me to a rush for a sorority on campus. I never saw myself as the sorority type, but I decided to go and see what it was about. I was impressed by the sisterhood and friendship I encountered. They spoke a lot about all of the community service work they were involved in and that was of great interest to me. I thought about it a few weeks and before I knew it, I was pledging a sorority. Having those sisters didn't replace the kind of love I have for my real sisters, but having them taught me a lot about myself. I learned that I'm not the odd one out having this secret story of a mother who didn't want me. There were times it made me feel like in the eyes of others, I was scarred in some way so I hardly ever told anyone that you'd left me when I was a baby. I now had my school work, cheerleading and I still played sports as well and along with that my new group of sisters, I was busy as we did our part to make sure the community that surrounded our school had our support, especially the local schools. We mentored younger girls and I was especially interested in helping and mentoring girls who didn't have a mother around because I could relate to how they were feeling. For the first time in my life, I shared my experiences of how I felt knowing my birth mother didn't want me and I could see that my heartfelt story was exactly what another young girl needed to help her with the same struggles I'd suffered through. I can't say that your absence was a good thing, but I can say that my story about the impact of your absence helped another young girl realize she too would be okay."

Chapter 23
Day 21, Age 21

"I tried to keep things together this year, but it was hard because Grandpa passed away this year. I knew something was going on when I looked up one day and my dad was visiting me on campus unannounced. When I saw him, he looked pained and I knew something was wrong. He had driven from Florida to Virginia to tell me and to console me and I found myself consoling him. They were very close as father and son and grandpa died unexpectedly from a massive heart attack.

He had been driving when it happened and was able to steer the car away from a crowd before the car came to a stop where he died before the ambulance even arrived. I rode back to Florida with dad and it gave us some time to reflect on many things.

We talked a little about you and he told me how grandpa was the one who tried to really help you when they found out you were pregnant with me. They didn't want dad's life to spiral downward because soon he would have to worry about how to take care of me and he was a college student. He told me grandpa saw to it that he never missed a beat in school and anything they could do for you they did.

Grandpa was the one who wanted dad to marry you, but daddy explained to me that what the two of you shared wasn't really the kind of love that would make for a good marriage and he didn't want to do it simply because you were pregnant with me. He wanted to do the right thing when he felt the time was right. He told me he felt like you were always holding something back from him, but he didn't know what it was. He made sure I knew that I was never, ever a mistake, but an unexpected blessing. When he finally made the decision to ask you to marry him, he said he did do it out of obligation and believed that in time, love would blossom.

I asked him did he try to look for you after you never returned to the house and he said in the beginning he tried to find you, but then realized he had a baby girl he had to look out for and care for and that was his priority.

This year was especially hard for the family, but we carried each other through it because that's what family does. When times get hard and rough, you don't run or walk away, but you stick together and hold on to each other. Whatever caused you to leave me so many years ago, I hope you didn't feel like you weren't wanted or that you didn't fit in with the family. They would have loved you. I know my family and they are loving and kind and would give their last, so whatever it was, I hope it was worth it and I hope it made you happy. I can't really hold any bad feelings toward you Rachel because the life I have is worth smiling about. I can also smile because finally, if nothing else, I think my being here is finally giving me the closure I've needed."

Chapter 24
Day 22, Age 22

"I graduated on time and it was a big day. First I took part in the graduation with all of the other students and then there was a special graduation for the students from the school of nursing. They had this tradition that each nursing student had to get other students to sign the nursing uniform that we had to wear our last year of school and then the day of graduation, we would string them across the lawn of the nursing building. I think daddy was more excited than I was because he must have taken a thousand pictures of my uniform as it hung proudly outside the school.

Lots of family came to Virginia for my graduation and rather than have any type of graduation party, I asked for a trip with the family so daddy, Anna and the twins and I spent two glorious weeks in Hawaii. The water was so blue and everything about Hawaii was so beautiful. One night I sat out on the beach and looked up at the stars and I actually talked to you. I remember speaking out loud and asking where you were and what were you doing. I asked over and over again why would you leave me and never come back. I wondered what kind of woman would do such a thing. I knew one day I wanted to have children of my own and for years I questioned what there was about me that you didn't like or that you didn't or couldn't love enough to stay.

That night I thought back over a lot of what I went through growing up and all I could think was that you didn't care anything about me at all. My heart bled for you on many occasions and I secretly mourned the mother I didn't have because I didn't want Anna to think she wasn't a good mother. She was and still is the best mother a girl could ask for. That didn't keep me from wondering why you left me a motherless child as an infant. I sat on the beach that night and wondered what could a child at one years of age have done that would make her mother not want to be a part of her life or even wonder what became of her.

I often wondered what became of you and all I can hope for is that somewhere over these years, you've thought about me enough to care that I had a good life. I am living a good and blessed life Rachel and despite years of wondering about you and never getting any answers, I can't say I would change anything because I don't want anything to take away from the life I've had with daddy, Anna and my sisters. I love them with all of my heart and I always want them to know it. What did you love so much back then that it took you away from me?"

Chapter 25
Day 23, Age 23

"My first day as a nurse was busy and exciting. I made the decision that I wanted to be a pediatric nurse and working with babies was the highlight of becoming a nurse. The love and care for those little lives is what I was meant to do.

When I first took the job and was offered the position in pediatrics, I wondered if it was because of the lack of having a mother in my life when I was little that I felt the need to care for a hurting child. I didn't have any of the health issues a lot of the babies who come to my floor have, but I felt and still feel a connection to them, wanting to be sure that there is always someone around to care for them. Parents can't be at the hospital twenty-four hours a day to sit with their children so I find it's my duty to provide the extra love and attention when the parents are not there. I don't have any children, but I have a nurturing spirit. I was born to be a caregiver. I think that a woman should never be a mother if she doesn't love being a caregiver. The first care they give that should be unconditional is the care of their own child. I don't know what your life was like growing up in foster care. Dad once told me that a lot of your childhood was spent going from one foster care home to another and he wasn't sure you'd ever really felt loved. Perhaps that had a lot to do with why you couldn't love me."

Houston stopped reading at that point. To her own ears she didn't like how that sounded. She shouldn't assume that Rachel didn't love her because she wasn't a mother to her. She remembered saying that once before when she was younger and her father sternly told her to never assume that Rachel didn't love her. He'd watched Rachel with me as a baby and he knew she loved me greatly and whatever decision she made, he had to believe her decision to leave me with him was what she did out of the enormous amount of love she had for me.

"I'm sorry Rachel. I shouldn't have said that because I don't know that you didn't love me. I only know that you weren't there. I look at how the children cry for their parents when they have to leave them at the hospital and my heart breaks. Those screams and cries make me want to do everything I can to make their stay at the hospital as comfortable as possible. I don't want them to feel abandoned and lonely because I know how that feels. My situation was different from theirs, but the feelings were similar. I became a nurse to help heal the hurt and soothe the abandoned and I take great pride in doing so."

Chapter 26
Day 24, Age 24

"I think I attract bad relationships like moths to a flame. I know it's bad from the start, yet I can't seem to pull myself away.

I went to Miami with some friends when I was twenty-four and while I was there I met a guy on the beach. He seemed nice though he was a few years older than me. My first sign that this may not be for me was because at twenty-nine, he was still trying to find himself. He was living on a friends couch, had dropped out of college to find himself and worked in a night club as a bartender. There is nothing wrong with any career, but he was all over the place with what he wanted to do in life.

We'd spent four days of having a lot of fun and when I returned home, we stayed in contact. Since I only lived a car ride away from Miami, he came to visit me often, borrowing a car from someone. When his visits became more and more frequent, I felt like he was moving closer to talking about us living together, something I would never, ever do. I have no issue with any woman who decides to do that, but that isn't for me. I would do that when a man placed a ring on my finger, says I do and makes a commitment to making our life together work, just as Noah has done.

This guy kept pressing and pressing me and when he realized I wouldn't allow him to move in with me, he became a stalker, calling all hours of the night to see if I was with someone and showing up without telling me he was coming to town. It got to the point where I had to take out an order to keep him away from me. I didn't tell my dad about this because I was afraid of what he would do. Eventually the guy got the message and never contacted me again, but it was a frightening time. I wasn't sure when I would look up and he would appear. He never threatened me in any way, but what he called love, I called obsession and the latter is not a way to have a healthy relationship. I was glad when he finally got over me and I never heard from him again. I knew then the type of relationship I wanted and I decided to wait it out until God sent me the man that was supposed to love me with unconditional and not obsessive love. That was a rough time, but just like in every other situation I've ever experienced, I survived."

Chapter 27
Day 25, Age 25

"I moved out of my apartment that I'd been living in since I started working at the hospital and bought a condo when I turned twenty-five. It was my first big purchase and thanks to my dad, I was able to put down a huge down payment to keep my mortgage at a rate that I could afford on my own. Of course I had to get one big enough to account for the large number of sleepovers I would have with my sisters.

They love hanging out with me and I love being able to give my dad and Anna free time together because these girls can be a handful. Anna helped me decorate it which was a lot of fun. We spent a lot of time shopping for just the right furniture, fixtures and window treatments. To my surprise, she gave the biggest house warming celebration and her gift to me was a portrait of the family that we'd taken a few years back that I still have hanging in my family room above the fireplace. Whenever I'm in that room, I look at it and remember how loved I am.

Buying my first home was a major milestone for me and I was thankful that my family was there to share in it with me. I think now of where I am, sitting here with you and realizing that soon our time will come to an end and you will never know about all of the wonderful achievements I've had in my life. Being here with you during this time is providing me with the chance to have the closure I have needed all these years, but it's not giving me any of the answers that I wished I could get from you. You'll leave here and though I finally see who you are, I don't know who you are, at least not for myself. I realize I will miss what I can't have from this time forward, more than I have missed what I didn't have with you in the past."

Chapter 28
Day 26, Age 26

"I met the love of my life this year. I walked into a coffee shop across the street from the hospital where I work, which I did every morning when I worked the early shift. This one morning the credit card machine was not working and the closest ATM machine was inside of the hospital. When the cashier told me the machine was down and I'd have to pay with cash, I knew that if I took the time to cross the street, go into the hospital to get cash from the ATM and then try to come back, I would be late for my shift. I was about to turn around when the man behind me handed the cashier a ten dollar bill to cover my coffee. Before I could tell him he didn't have to do that, he stopped me and said not to worry because it was the gentlemanly thing to do. When he said, "please let me buy you a cup of coffee," I couldn't say no after looking into his eyes.

He was handsome and strong looking and when he smiled, my heart melted. I couldn't speak so I nodded. While we stood to the side waiting for our coffees, I then found the words to thank him for the coffee. I offered to return the money if he told me where I could send it. He laughed and I swear my whole world lit up from him jubilance. He told me there was no need because he happily bought a pretty woman a coffee and it was well worth every penny even on an intern's menial salary. I asked if he was an intern at the hospital and he said it was his first day. I told him I was a nurse at the hospital and I congratulated him and wished him well.

We grabbed our coffees and walked across the street together. He told me his name was Noah and after telling him my name, we talked about all the things I knew about the city that I was named after. He was surprised that I knew everything about Houston, Texas which was where my parents first met.

That was a few years ago and last year, he asked me to marry him and I said yes. In fact, we were supposed to be getting married at the end of this month, but we postponed the wedding so that I could come here and get some closure on a part of my life that has been a mystery to me.

A wedding is considered to be one of the most exciting times in a girl's life and every girl wants to be able to share in that moment with her mother. Anna is excited and I'm excited that she's excited. It only reminds me that you're here in this hospital, in this bed and I'm saying goodbye because we only have a few days left to spend together. My life will go on, I will marry Noah, have children and I just realized I will have nothing much to share with them about you and that makes me sad. This should not be all that there is between a woman and the child she gave birth to. Hello and goodbye should never occur this close together."

Chapter 29
Day 27, Age 27

"Grandma passed away this year and I was heartbroken like nothing I'd ever felt before. We were very close and after I graduated college and moved back to Florida, I spent a lot of time with her.

After grandpa passed away, she seemed sad and lonely and daddy tried to get her to move into the house with him and Anna, but she refused, not wanting to leave the house that she shared her life in with grandpa. It was difficult with her living in Texas while we were all in Florida, but she insisted she was fine. After she experienced a fall that prevented her from being able to walk for a month, she finally moved to Florida and in with dad, Anna and my sisters and her spirits were lifted being around family again.

I had moved into my condo and when I needed my alone time, the condo provided that. When I wasn't working or spending time with the family or Noah, I was with grandma making sure she didn't have time to wallow in sorrow because she missed grandpa. We went shopping and to the movies and I even talked her into doing more fun things with some friends she'd made once she moved to Florida. A few times, my dad even flew her friends to Florida so that she could still feel connected to them. When they got together, they had more fun than my friends and I would have. There was no boring bingo or days of sitting around and crocheting with friends.

Grandma learned how to paint and a few times I had to pick her up from sip and paint nights out because she'd had a few sips too many. She started going to some of the dances at the senior center and some man had even been sniffing around her. They had become great companions for each other and I was happy to see her happy again because family means everything to me. I only had that one side of the family to enjoy because I knew nothing about your life.

Once daddy told me the story of how he met you and where you lived. I visited that street one day when I was twenty-seven because I wanted to see if the house where you lived in foster care was still there. This was around the time that we packed up the house in Texas to move grandma to Florida. I had been in Texas a few days and decided to look for the house where you lived back when you'd met my dad. The strange thing is a few of the older people who still lived on the street saw me and told me that I reminded them of someone, but that they couldn't place where. I didn't have the nerve to walk up to the house where you lived to ask about you because I figured if they knew where you were, then you should have been around to ask about me. At that age, I figured if you were still alive, I wouldn't want to impose on your privacy. You'd preferred it all along and I wouldn't think of disturbing that.

I never told daddy I went driving by that house. After all those years, I'm sure he was hoping that I would have gotten over the fact that you walked away, but I realized that day that I never did. The ghost of who I thought you were never left me and the visual of who you were haunted me until the first day I walked into this hospital and saw you. You're no longer a ghost, but you're still someone I don't know and it saddens me that these one way conversations that I have from notes I write the night before are all the time I will get. I thought not having you or knowing you would be the hardest thing, but now I realize knowing about you, seeing you, but not having you is even worse."

Chapter 30
Day 28, Age 28

"I got engaged when I was twenty-eight and it seems everyone was in on it, but me; even the twins. Out of the blue, Anna decided to have this big elaborate dinner at the house. She's always been the type of mother to cook, but even this was overboard for her.

This was a dinner with a five course meal and on the menu were all of my favorite things. I had invited Noah, but he said he had plans with his family that he couldn't change. We sat down for dinner in the dining room which was something we seldom did, deciding most times to eat around the kitchen table. Everyone was very talkative and kept looking around like they were expecting something. Unbeknownst to me, in the back yard of the house, Noah and his family had set up the scene for a romantic proposal and when dinner was over, dad asked me to make sure the back door to the house was locked. When I went into the kitchen I could see that there was a lot of lights in the back yard. I opened the door and there on his knees in the back yard was Noah surrounded by his parents, brothers, sister and their spouses. Someone turned on music and over some speakers I heard what I knew was our song which was "He Loves Me" by Jill Scott. My family came out and stood behind Noah with his family as he shared how much he loved me and what it has meant to him to have me as a part of his life. I cried like a baby and could barely get out my answer which of course was yes because he turned out to be the man of my dreams; the man of every woman's dreams."

Chapter 31
Day 29, Age 29

"Planning for the wedding has been great fun. This whole year everyone in my family has been giving all of their attention to making sure my wedding is perfect. I thought I would be stressed, but I wasn't at all. Anna has been a great help and a staunch supporter. I think my sisters are more excited than even I am especially knowing they're going to be bridesmaids.

One day Noah caught me in a melancholy mood and asked me what was wrong because he'd called my name several times and I had completely zoned out. I told him I was again thinking about you and what was going on in your life. He sat down and let me vent about the times in my life when I longed for you simply because you'd given birth to me and not because of anything I was lacking. In a year I would be taking a walk down the aisle to be joined with Noah in marriage and in a life time of love and still I felt a little empty because deep down I wanted you to show up and sit on the front row of the church and smile and cry as I said my vows.

I've never been more loved than what I feel from my family, friends, Noah and his family and yet something is still missing. It's like the never-ending story that offers no closure. I remember feeling and wondering about how can I finally close this chapter of my life; the part where I still long for a mother when my deepest feelings are telling me she doesn't care. If she did, in all these years she could have made an attempt to reach out and at least explain leaving me full of want."

Houston put her book down, no longer wanting to read, but felt the need to talk directly to her.

"Rachel, didn't you have any feelings at all that one day I would long for you; long for answers that only you could provide? To find that you have been alive and well all these years just leaves me with more questions and pains me even more. You went off and started a new life and never looked back. It couldn't have been that you didn't want children because you have Mark and I've talked to him a few times over the past couple of days as he tries to get here within the next day or so. He loves you, Marcus loves you, Lana loves you and all of the friends who have been keeping vigil at your beside have the greatest love and adoration for you, so the heartless woman I've wanted to believe you were is not the woman they all know and love, so who are you?

Noah and I sat up for hours that night a year ago and I spilled all of my heartache and when I was done he told me to let it go. He didn't want me taking any ill-willed feelings into our marriage especially when I didn't know what drew you away, but he wanted to pray that whatever it was that it was the right decision for you and that I would be able to forgive you for it because our lives together could never be whole if I continued to walk around in a state of unrest that has lasted for almost thirty years. I didn't have a major event when I was twenty-nine, but I want you to know that even at that age, as I was preparing to marry the man I love, I still thought of you."

Chapter 32
Day 30, Age 30

To say that her legs were shaky would be an understatement, Houston thought to herself. As she walked toward Rachel's room, she felt like the hallway was getting longer and longer. Her feelings about the day confused her. She felt a connection to Rachel she never thought she would feel as she thought back to the first day she'd arrived at the hospital. Today, she knew, would be a long day because it was the day before the hospital would be turning off Rachel's life support and she wasn't sure how she should feel.

Over the past month, she'd changed and where she thought she was taking thirty days to say goodbye to Rachel, she was saying hello to herself. She'd spent a lot of years wrapped up in wonder and the not knowing when it came to Rachel that the feeling of peace that was now settling over her was unexpected. She walked into Rachel's room and the nurses had put a beautiful purple and silver gown on Rachel and even in the state that she was in, her beautiful showed through all of the bandages, wires and tubes.

"We don't have much time left to spend together Rachel and I couldn't think of anything that happened this year that I really wanted to highlight other than the feelings I experienced when I was told what happened to you.

My first feeling was shock at knowing that you were alive all these years. Next there was delight knowing you had not died at an early age, but had been alive. Then there was worry over whether or not you were experiencing pain that even medication couldn't help. Then up next was hurt that you apparently knew how to find me, but didn't. I wondered how long had you known where I was and if there was ever a time when you wanted to make your presence known and try to make amends. I would have been open to it. I may have been hesitant in the beginning, but eventually I would have welcomed you with open arms because that's the kind of person my dad raised me to be. The feeling I hated the most was anger, not just at you, but at God as well. I couldn't understand how He could not intervene and make it so that you and I could have crossed paths at a time when we could sit and talk through my years of hurt and disappointment. Along with all of those feelings came the feeling of want. I wanted to get to California as quickly as I could if for no other reason than to say goodbye to you. I was filled with so many emotions that now I feel blessed.

I'm thankful for the opportunity to have had this little bit of time with you. If this is what I was meant to have then I accept it knowing that I can't choose the path that you decided to walk starting thirty years ago, but I can forgive what that choice left me with and now I leave that all in my past. I now know that I will be a better me because I can now move on."

Chapter 33
Day 31

"Well Rachel, today is the day. I came early today because at five o'clock this evening, the hospital is going to turn off the machine that continues to breathe for you.

I can't believe I've been here for thirty days and I must say that I'm going to be okay. When I first heard you were here and I decided to come, I didn't know what would come of my visit. My original plan was to spend a few days and then go back to my life in Florida. Then the day before I left, I decided I wanted to stay until the end to see this all the way through. I'm glad I decided to stay this long. God knew I needed to find some peace with this and I think I have that now.

I don't think I can stick around until five o'clock because I don't want to watch them pull the plug on your life. We've missed thirty years together and now we will miss the next thirty years as well and I can't stand here and watch you slip away from me yet again knowing how final that would be. I've had my closure and I've done what I set out to do, but watching you take your last breath is something I'm not sure I can handle. I can't let that be the last remnant of what I remember about you. I wanted a few moments alone with you to finally say goodbye and to let you know that I was here. Sleep well into eternity Rachel and God willing, we will see each other one day."

Houston leaned down and kissed Rachel's cheek and as she leaned up, a tear from her own eye fell and landed on Rachel's face. She started to wipe it off, but instead, she left it there and stood still as she watched it dry into her skin. That small tear would be a part of her that Rachel will always have.

She gave one last look at the woman who gave her life and she turned and walked away. As she walked, she thought about her decision to not stay and to also not return for Rachel's funeral. She knew it was time to return to her life in Florida.

Chapter 34

As she pulled up to the house, Houston could see that Marcus was leaving to head to the hospital for his own final goodbye to the woman he'd loved for the past thirty years. She already felt a sense of grief for him and what he was about to do and prayed that he would be given the strength to endure the pain.

He walked over to her as she exited the car.

"So you decided to not stay until five o'clock?" he asked.

Rachel didn't want him to think that she was choosing now to abandon Rachel in some symbolic way of how Rachel had abandoned her so many years ago. She couldn't handle what was to come and wasn't ashamed to admit it.

"I've spend the last thirty days with Rachel and I've released so much hurt, anger and frustration that I've felt for her for so many years and the thought of standing there while she took her last breath wasn't sitting well with me. I think I've said enough and I've said goodbye and prayed that God would grant her a peaceful journey into heaven. I'm going to pack and tomorrow morning, I'm going to fly back to Florida. Thank you for your hospitality. I don't think I can thank you enough for the kindness you've shown me. I hope you can understand my need to leave now."

Marcus reached out and placed a comforting hand on her shoulder.

"I understand more than you know. How did the open letter to her go for the past thirty days that I know you've been writing? I hoped it helped to get out everything you wanted to say."

"I'm thankful for them. All of my life, I've had events that any girl would want to share with her mother and though Rachel wasn't around, it gave me comfort being able to share the last thirty years of my life with her even though she couldn't hear it. My dad was right when he said I needed to come and that the idea of the thirty days of sharing thirty years would be healing for me because he knew of my life-long struggles not knowing her."

"Rachel never, ever stopped thinking about you. It was a hard subject for her throughout our marriage. I had hoped that your time with her this past month would heal your broken heart. Though no one can ever say they know how you felt or even how Rachel felt all these years, I won't try to explain her decisions to you, but I will say, leaving you was hard for her and she had regret that ate away at her for many years."

Marcus moved to stand next to her as they leaned on the car.

"I found something that belonged to Rachel that I think you should have. For many years, she kept a box that was labeled, Houston, and she made me promise to never ever touch it because it was her personal world, her own space that she never wanted invaded by anyone. I don't know what she kept in that box and I never violated her trust by attempting to see what was in it. She kept the box stored in the lower level of the house in a closet that had nothing in it but that box. I pulled it out today and I left it for you. I will leave it up to you to decide what to do with it, but I think at this point, it would be okay if you opened it, but only if you want to. I know you'll be packing to leave so think about it. It's just eleven o'clock and I have a few errands to run before I head to the hospital in a few hours to be there at five o'clock when they'll turn off the ventilator so if you need me, you know how to reach me, otherwise, I'll see you this evening. I'm also expecting Mark sometime today. The last word I got was he was on a flight and should be here in about an hour. I'm glad you'll get to meet him before you leave."

Houston didn't react because for a few seconds, she thought her heart had stopped beating. Rachel had kept a box with her name on it and no one knew the contents. Marcus knew her struggles for the past thirty days and wanted to provide her with as much comfort as he could and not knowing what was in the box, he left it up to her to decide what to do.

"Thank you Marcus. My dad said he talked to you several times over the past month and that he knew you were a good man. He also told me last night that you apologized to him because thirty years ago, Rachel left him and I in order to be with you, but that you didn't know about me back then. He said Rachel didn't tell you about me until ten years later. She was young and immature when she had me and she did what she felt she needed to do being the person that she was back then. It took my dad a lot of years to get over her leaving us, especially me being an infant. Rather than spill words of hatred and despair about Rachel, he filled my life with love and comfort and he said that it wasn't up to him to try and tell Rachel's story because he didn't know it. Now we'll never know it, but at least, I got the chance to see her and hear about her life all these years, from you. Thank you for telling me about the box."

"Okay, well I'm going to head out. Ms. Sophia left some food warming for you in the oven and if you want something else, she's around to make you whatever you want. I'll call and check on you later and if you change your mind about being at the hospital later, we'll be there to support you if you want to be there. I hope you'll consider my son and I family now. He'll be arriving around noon and will be heading straight to the hospital, but we'll both be home later this evening after I've taken care of everything. We won't know the outcome, but whatever it is, before you go back to Florida, I'd like you, Mark and I to sit down and talk."

"I look forward to it and I'm glad to hear he'll make it in time to say goodbye to his mother. I've spoken with him twice and I look forward to meeting him later. I have two younger sisters, but I've never had a brother. He's twenty-two right?"

"Yes and he'll be twenty-three next month. He's been in the Navy since he turned eighteen following in my footsteps. He has wanted to be in the Navy since he was a little boy and never spoke of anything but that. We're very proud of him and he and his mother are very close, so I know this will be hard on him. I'm glad you're here and I hope the two of you can lean on each other."

Houston nodded as a lump formed in her throat. The weight of how much she'd missed in thirty years was coming down on her. She couldn't speak, afraid she'd start crying.

"You go ahead in and continue to make yourself at home and make sure you eat. Ms. Sophia said she didn't think you ate anything last night or this morning before you left. Your father wouldn't be happy to hear that I'm letting you starve," Marcus said, lighting the mood.

Houston did smile then and walked toward the house while waving to him as he left.

As she entered the house, her only thought was on getting to the box that had her name on it. She used the temporary key that Marcus had given her and as soon as she entered the foyer, sitting on a table at the foot of the winding staircase was a huge box labeled, 'Houston'. She stared at it, unable to move her feet to reach out for it.

"Houston, you're back!" she heard Ms. Sophia say.

"Yes, Ms. Sophia. I've already been to the hospital and thought I'd come back to lie down for a while before I packed."

"Don't you lie down before you get something to eat. Mr. Marcus gave me strict instructions that I was to be sure you ate a good meal when you returned. I know you like Italian food so I have lasagna warming in the oven and I've made a nice salad and some fresh garlic rolls. Shall I fix you a plate now?" she asked.

Houston had fallen in love with Ms. Sophia from the first day they'd met. She reminded her of her own grandmother she'd lost many years ago.

"That sounds yummy. I'll be right in the kitchen," she said, turning once again back to the box.

She watched as Ms. Sophia turned toward the kitchen as she reached for the box. It wasn't very heavy so she carried it with her.

"Why don't you sit at the table to eat if you plan to go through that box now? I'll get your food and bring it to you."

Houston sat at the table and placed the box on the floor beside her. She waited a few minutes as her fingers nervously twitched in anticipation of what the box held. Ms. Sophia placed a huge helping of lasagna and rolls in front of her along with a big plate of salad.

She said grace and dug in, hoping a little food to start off with would help ease her nervousness. After getting a taste of the mouth-watering lasagna, she finally got up the nerve to open the box. She reached down and opened the flaps holding it together and looked inside before reaching. What she saw were several notebooks with dates on them. She reached in and lifted a few and noticed that there were ten of them in all and each had a time frame where if put together, they would span her entire thirty year life. She removed them and placed them on the table beside her. She then looked into the box again and inside was a shoebox and when she opened the lid to it, inside was a big stack of photos. When her stomach began to growl from hunger, she decided to finish her meal first and then concentrate on the contents of the box, giving it her full attention.

After finishing the salad and using the last smidgeon of bread to wipe the remnants of the delicious lasagna from her plate, she turned her attention to the items within the box.

She looked at the notebooks and laid them out in date order in front of her. She then opened the first notebook that was dated from the year she was born until she was four years old. When she opened the first notebook, the inscription inside read, "A Letter to My Daughter". Houston didn't move as the words leapt from the page at her. Rachel had written to her. She turned the page and began reading. The tears began rolling down her face after she read the first paragraph.

Many years ago, Rachel had begun writing to her to explain about the choices she made when at nineteen years old, she ran away from the child she loved more than life itself and from a man whom she didn't know well and who wasn't the love of her life though they'd been close. Though having Houston was not a mistake, the life that she wanted was with Marcus who was in the Navy and who was finally going to send for her.

She'd met Houston's father and liked him immediately, but she didn't tell him that she had a boyfriend who was in the Navy. Her father and Rachel were dating and having fun when she'd gotten pregnant with her. While reading further, she discovered that Rachel had been living in foster care and never knew what it meant to love and commit to a child. At that time, Houston's dad was twenty years old, and had been home for the summer from college when they'd met. By the end of the summer, Rachel was pregnant and the foster family told her she had to leave, especially since she was eighteen and they weren't getting any money for her anymore. Since Rachel was pregnant with her, her father's family took Rachel in to help with the baby so that her dad could continue his studies at a college nearby.

Back then, they were living in Houston, Texas where her grandfather owned a law firm that specialized in corporate law. Her father's family never cared much for Rachel thinking she wasn't good enough to be a part of their family, but because they loved Houston's father, they did what they had to do in order to care for the baby Rachel was carrying.

For almost a year after Houston was born, her parents tried to make it work. Secretly, Rachel was still in contact with Marcus who was from the same neighborhood where she lived as a foster child. She had been in love with Marcus since she was fifteen and when he went into the navy, she felt lonely and unloved since Marcus was the only person who cared about her. When she'd met Houston's dad, he showered her with the love and attention she craved.

One day when Houston was about ten months old, she'd gone to visit Marcus' family and was told that he had been trying to find her. None of them knew she had been pregnant with Houston. They only knew that one day she'd disappeared. Being young and immature and still longing for Marcus, she took the number given to her to reach him and they began talking daily on the phone while Houston's dad was away at school during the day and at work in the evenings.

While talking to Marcus he'd told her of the dream life they would have if she came with him. He would be spending a lot of time away since he was in the Navy, but he would set her up in base housing and they could finally have a good life together. She'd never told him about the baby that wasn't his and she wasn't sure he'd accept her and the baby. She then made the dumbest and hardest mistake she'd ever made in her life. When Houston's dad had come home one day from class and not having to work that evening, he wanted to take her and Rachel out for some family time and to talk about him and Rachel getting married. She knew that Marcus was coming for her any day and she had a decision to make; should she stay with Houston and Nick, her dad, or should she go with Marcus. Realizing she wasn't ready to be a mother and that she still loved Marcus, she told Nick she was running to the store to get something nice to wear for their family day out. While Nick was playing with Houston, Rachel went to her room and filled a large duffel bag with as many clothes as she could fit into it. She left a note telling Nick that she was sorry, but that she couldn't stay and that Houston would have a much better life with him and his family. She left out of the back door of the house and never looked back. She never stopped thinking about Houston, but once she'd made the decision to leave and had actually done so, she couldn't change her mind. She took the plane ticket that Marcus had sent to his parent's house and she flew out to California where she lived her life far from Texas. She spent years living out of the country as well with Marcus moving around a lot, but they always considered California their home.

Houston read page after page in book after book and never stopped crying the whole time. Her mother had shared with her every aspect of her life from the day she left and didn't leave anything out.

The books really started getting interesting when Houston came across passages that spoke of events in Houston's life that it seems Rachel had been at. She read passages about Rachel sneaking into the back of the elementary school auditorium to watch Houston at age seven in her first play and flute recital. She recalled the time when at age eight, Houston had her birthday party at a horse farm and then in the margin, there was a note that said, 'picture in box from party'.

Houston remembered the box of photos and opened it wondering what she would find. Inside were stacks and stacks of photos that spanned her life from childhood until she graduated from college. How could this be? she thought. Where did Rachel get pictures of her over all those years? She flipped through them and a lot were of Rachel through the years and there were just as many of Houston. Had Rachel had someone take these pictures or had she been there for all of these events. There were pictures of her when she first began playing volleyball at age nine. She saw pictures from swimming competitions and from football games where she was a cheerleader from middle school all the way through high school. There was even a picture of her leaving her prom as she got into a limousine to head to the after party at the local bowling alley. There were pictures from step competitions she had been in after she pledged a sorority in college. She even found several of her taken from a distance at her college graduation. There had to be hundreds of pictures of her over the years that she'd never seen before. She turned back to the notebooks hoping to find out more.

Houston found that she couldn't read fast enough. Rachel's writings mesmerized her and it was clear that she had been on her mind her entire life. Rachel had done what she thought was best for Houston and Houston had to admit that she lived a wonderful life. Her grandparents had showered her with more than enough love and affection and her father always showed and told her how much he loved her. She never wanted for anything.

Houston looked at the time and realized she had been sitting for hours reading and looking at pictures. The clock on the wall now read four o'clock in the afternoon, just an hour before Rachel would finally slip away forever.

She closed the book she was reading for a moment and closed her eyes in prayer asking God to give her the strength to continue reading. All of her senses were overwhelmed by the love that radiated from the pages from Rachel to her. She gave herself a minute to breathe and the last book in the stack caught her attention because it was the only one that did not have an ending year on it. She bypassed all the others and opened that one book. The beginning date was just one year ago so she opened it. Most of the pages were empty as she flipped through them. She turned to the last several pages of words which were dated the night before the car accident that caused Rachel to be in a coma. She turned to the first page of that night before and she began to read.

"Well Houston, this is it. I haven't told anyone this, not even Marcus, but I think it's time. I've suffered for thirty years and rightly so after robbing you of having

me as your mother in your life. I know that your step-mother has been wonderful to you and I don't discount that. I know that she loves you as much as any woman could love a daughter. I've watched you from a distance for many years. There were years when I didn't even tell Marcus that I would fly into Texas just so that I could get a glimpse of you. When you moved from Texas to Florida, I would visit there too. Marcus was a career Naval officer, so he was gone a lot and during a lot of those times, after hiring a private detective to keep up with you and your father, I would catch red-eye flight and go to Texas to watch your recitals or to watch your games when you played sports and even cheer along with you as you cheered on squads for years.

After I had my son, the guilt of leaving you would not let up and I would either have the private eye take pictures for me or I would come myself so that I could feel some part of being in your life or at least being in your corner. I didn't know if I would ever get up the nerve to ask your father if I could finally meet you, but I'm going to do that tomorrow.

I have been very active in civic organizations and there is a conference that starts tomorrow in Florida and it's only an hour's drive from where you and your father live. I'm planning on attending the conference and hopefully I'll get the chance to speak to your father, to beg for the chance to talk to you. I didn't want to approach you without his permission so that it wouldn't be too much of a blow. I haven't contacted him yet, for fear that he would say no if I asked over the phone. I'm hoping doing so in person would be less of a negative sting. I know Marcus would support me in my desire to finally see you and explain to you what happened all those years ago, but just in case it doesn't work out, I don't want him burdened with trying to soothe my despair if your father's answer is no. If he says no, I won't go against his wishes because I have no right to. All I can do is beg for his forgiveness and plead with him for a chance to see and talk to you even if all you want to tell me is to continue to stay out of your life. Houston, I'm sorry for all the missed years, events and times we could have spent as mother and daughter. Many, many times I've thought that if I would be granted the opportunity to go back to the day I thoughtlessly left you, what would I do differently.

I would never have left the way that I did. I would have explained to Marcus that I'd met your father and had you and hoped that he would still want me. I knew then just as I know now that he would have accepted you with open arms, but at nineteen years old, the last thing I was doing was thinking. I would still have left you with Nick because I still believe that was the right decision. The wrong decision was walking away and not working things out where I could still be a part of your life. Shared custody happens every day and knowing the kind-hearted person your dad is, I think he would have been hurt at first, but understanding at the same time. I should have been honest with him and Marcus back then and I wasn't and my punishment for my foolish behavior was not having a daughter as wonderful as you in my life. I've missed out on the first thirty years of your life and I realize I don't want to miss anymore if you give me the chance.

I want you to know that you have a brother named Mark and I've told him about you and the mistake I made years ago walking away from you and he said, he hoped he could meet you someday and that you'll forgive me enough to want to have a relationship with us. He's never had any siblings and thinks he would love having a sister. I never told him or my husband that I've kept track of you all these years, but I plan to do that once I return from Florida, hopefully with good news that you at least agreed to meet with me while I was there. I don't know what the outcome of tomorrow will hold, but I trust God and tomorrow will turn out the way He has planned it to be.

I've prayed for forgiveness and I believe God has granted me that. I've been praying daily that God will soften the heart of your dad and that he will hear me out and allow me the chance to make amends. I've prayed for you daily since the day I left and when I really learned to pray and knew how to pray, I made sure God knew I meant every single word of each prayer I prayed for you, that he would keep you safe and that you would always know love in your life, something I didn't have growing up.

I've been writing to you for the past thirty years, not knowing if or when I'd ever get to see and talk to you, but I wanted to be sure that I if so, I kept a record over the years so that I could share my life with you and hope that you would do the same with me.

I'm anxious and excited all at the same time, but I know if I don't do this tomorrow, I probably will not get up the nerve to do it again so, as I stated at the beginning, this is it. I'm coming to hopefully see you and I pray that tomorrow can be the beginning of a new start for us both. I have an early morning flight and I'm sure I won't get much sleep tonight, but with the long flight, I'll try and get some sleep on the plane. I'm hoping that this is my last letter to you , praying that after tonight, we'll be able to talk and I won't need to write everything down anymore. Until tomorrow, this is hopefully, my final letter in writing to you, my precious Houston. Love, Rachel.

Houston stood up sharply. Her feet felt heavy, her legs were wobbly and she grabbed her chest at the pain she felt in her heart.

Rachel had been suffering for thirty years with a pain that no one should ever feel. There was still more that she needed to read, but she'd read enough to know that for thirty years, she thought that her mother didn't love her and never wanted her when in fact, she did what she knew was best for her knowing that in her heart she couldn't stay. She could have just as easily taken Houston and run away, but she didn't because she knew that wouldn't be a life for either one of them to live and Rachel also knew that Houston's father loved her and Rachel didn't want to tear that away from him.

For thirty years, the woman who gave birth to her loved her, prayed for her daily and kept a watchful eye over her. There was no hatred for her or for her dad as she sometimes thought Rachel may have had. She wasn't off living her life, never, ever thinking about Houston and what she'd become. She didn't keep the secret from her husband, son and best friend, but she told them of the mistake she'd made years ago and they supported her through the years of torment that she must have suffered through.

Houston was hurting for her mother, not because she had been in an accident and was in a coma, but because her mother spent years as a child feeling unloved and unwanted and she was never taught how to love a child at a young age and where she could have made an even bigger mistake by running with Houston, she put Houston first and made the right choice when she knew she had a choice she had to make. It couldn't have been easy and Houston couldn't continue to harbor any hurt or anger.

Her mother was lying in a hospital bed, less than an hour away from taking her last breath and she wasn't there. Houston fell to her knees not knowing what else to do, but pray the way she was taught by her dad as a child.

"She'll be alone and without me in her last hours. God I'm so sorry for my selfish attitude. I know the choices she made could not have been easy and I am about to make one as well. No one should have had to endure the life she had as a child growing up or having to make the choice that she had to make and living with thirty years of regret. Soften my heart God and let me do what I know I should do, not out of obligation, but out of love for the woman who gave me life. I've missed thirty years with her God, please don't let me miss her last few moments. Forgive me for not honoring her with my presence when she now needs me the most. Forgive me for walking away on this last day when I should be standing tall and strong for her when she needs me. I thank you for providing that ram in the bush in the form of my step-mother when you did because I didn't grow up without a mother figure in my life. I give all honor to you for blessing my life and the life of my mother and whatever your will is, I trust you and I love you, Amen."

Houston stood and glanced at the clock. It was now four-forty five, and in fifteen minutes, her mother will be gone. Without thinking, she grabbed her keys and purse and sprinted for the door. The hospital was over twenty minutes away, but she prayed as she drove safely, asking God to not take her mother before she got to the hospital.

Chapter 35

Houston arrived at the hospital at five fifteen. She cried as she ran from the car through the hospital to get to Rachel. She didn't wait for the elevator, but sprinted up four flights, not wanting to waste any time. As she ran down the hall toward the room, she could see Marcus at Rachel's bedside, her mom's best friend Lana was there and next to Lana was a young man dressed in military attire and she assumed that was her brother. What surprised her most was the fact that as she got closer to the room, she also saw her father and her fiancé, Noah. Seeing them made her rush even harder and as she got to the room, she rushed into her father's waiting arms and cried.

"Is she gone Daddy?" she cried.

"No, they haven't turned the equipment off yet. Her doctor wanted to be here and he is running a few minutes behind, so we're just waiting on him."

"What are you and Noah doing here? When did you get here?"

"We flew out this morning. We've been trying to call you all morning, but you haven't been answering your phone. Marcus said you were at the house and wasn't sure you were coming."

Houston realized she never took her phone out of her purse and she'd gotten so engrossed in her mother's writing that she never thought of it. She turned to Noah and embraced and kissed him, thankful that she was blessed with a man who had no problem putting everything on hold to be here for her.

"Thank you for coming. You always know when I need you. I love you so much," she said to him, still holding on to him tight.

"I love you too baby and I wouldn't be anywhere else, but by your side," he responded.

Houston then turned to who she assumed was her brother.

"I assume you're Mark?" she asked him.

He smiled, shook his head yes and extended his hand to her. She looked at it and knew it wouldn't be enough. Before she thought about her action, she reached out and pulled him into a hug so tight she feared she'd cut his breathing off. She couldn't believe how happy she was to meet him after hearing about him from Marcus and talking to him a few times on the phone.

"I'm so happy to meet you and a handshake with my brother wasn't going to be enough," she said through tears that were now staining her cheeks.

After hugging Lana and Marcus as well, Houston went close to the bed, thankful that God saw fit for her to be here at her mother's end if that was his will.

The room was quiet as they waited for the doctor to enter. Houston leaned down and kissed Rachel on the cheek and held back more tears that were threatening to fall as she spoke.

"I'm right here Mommy. If you can hear me, I am right here and I'm not going anywhere as long as you're here too. I read most of your letters to me and I saw the pictures and I want you to know that there is nothing that you need my forgiveness for. If you have to go now, you go ahead and go into God's waiting arms knowing that I love you, Mark and I will always have each other and Marcus now has a pesky step-daughter that he will never, ever get rid of. You have your wish and God granted your prayer that we would be together and though you may not be here with us, we now have each other because of you."

Houston kissed her one last time before she looked up and noticed the doctor and a nurse had entered. The doctor explained what would occur once they disconnected the machines and that they weren't sure how long she would hold on breathing on her own, but that it was the wish of her husband that they not prolong her life if it wasn't her breath that was going in and out. Rachel wouldn't want a machine breathing for her.

Everyone shook their heads in agreement as Marcus signed the papers allowing the hospital to turn off the breathing machine.

She reached out for Mark's hand as they stood together over Rachel and waited for God's will.

The family stood around for almost an hour before Rachel's labored breathing finally stopped. The one machine that monitored life signs beeped with a long signal letting them know that Rachel had flat-lined and had passed away.

Everyone hugged each other as each gave Rachel one last kiss, including her father who also had tears in his eyes. There was no room for hatred or anger and none existed.

"I love you Mommy," Houston said before moving into Noah's arms who stood and held her, giving her the comfort he knew she needed.

After each person was done the doctor moved toward the machine to turn off the loud piercing sound when just before he reached for the switch, the machine beeped. Where the machine had moments before showed signs of no life, everyone turned to the screen and noticed the once flat line was now showing a signal of a heartbeat. One short beep turned into several short beats and Houston noticed Rachel's chest rising and falling. She was trying to breathe. She moved to the side of the bed at the same time as Marcus.

"My God, she's breathing!" Houston exclaimed.

"Yes!" Mark shouted.

"That's it baby, come on back to me," Marcus cheered.

"Come on Rachel, you can do it," Nick hollered.

"That's it, breathe Rachel, keep on breathing," Lana screamed.

The doctor checked her over and the nurse asked everyone to step back from the bed so that they could examine her. As they took her vitals everyone stood waiting to see what was going on.

After ten long minutes of the doctor and nurses talking to Rachel encouraging her to open her eyes, she did, not looking at anyone in particular, but she looked up at the ceiling.

"Rachel, can you hear me?" the doctor asked. He then grabbed her hand and placed his inside of hers.

"If you can hear me, I need you to squeeze my hand. Can you do that?" he asked.

Everyone looked down at her hand that was holding his and notice a slight movement. After a few seconds, she did it again.

He pulled out a miniature light and flashed it across her eyes.

"Rachel, can you follow this light with your eyes for me?"

She again followed his instruction and followed the light with her eyes and then turning her head slightly to follow the light even more.

"That's it Mommy, you can do it. God's got a plan for a new beginning and it starts today," Houston said anxious to come closer, but staying back, following instructions. She was a nurse herself and she knew how important it was to let the doctor and nurse check her over.

"Rachel, I see that you can turn your head slightly. Can you nod a little for me?"

She was able to do that also and the doctor smiled.

"Okay, now Rachel, you have a tube that I'm going to remove that we've been using to feed you and another that was helping you to breath. You're going to feel uncomfortable for a few minutes, but I think it's time to take them out so bear with us."

The doctor pushed the call button on the wall and called for additional help and suddenly the room flooded with doctors and nurses going about making sure they checked her thoroughly.

"Listen, why don't we all step out and regroup to allow the doctors to do what they need to do to assess Rachel's condition," Lana said.

Without questioning, everyone followed Marcus out and hugged again with joy and excitement that Rachel was breathing on her own.

"Now this is what it means to stand back and watch God work," Marcus said to the group.

"As much as we were all ready to let her go because it's been a rough month, I can truly say that I'm thankful for a God who gives us second chances. He proved today that not every doctor has the answer when He's in control!" Lana added.

"Let's say a prayer of thanks right now," Nick said and everyone joined heads and bowed while he prayed.

"Thank you God for your mercy and your grace. Thank you for doing something that we know only you can do. We thank you for Rachel's life as you continue to guide the hand of the doctors as they follow the path you've already put in place. We are a family that loves and trusts you and we don't take it for granted that you have given us more time with Rachel. This is a time to heal old wounds and begin a new walk keeping you as the center. We ask now that you continue to cover us all and create a bond that nothing can break. We give you praise and honor because we know you are a God who doesn't make mistakes. For all of our health and strength, in the name of your Son, we say amen and thank you."

By the time he was finished with the prayer and everyone looked up, the doctor was exiting Rachel's room.

"Rachel is now fully awake and aware of her surroundings. She doesn't remember the accident, but she knows she's in the hospital and has been her for a little over a month. She can talk a little though her words come out a little scratchy due to the tube that's been in. Her talking will improve as her throat heals. For now, you can all go in to see her. We've set her up a little in bed and even with a scratchy throat she's asking for Houston and Mark.

"She's asking for me?" Houston asked.

"Yes and every time we ask her a question and she answers, she asks where you and Mark are. We told her you were here and that we would get you as soon as we were finished. She's very weak, but she is adamant about the fact that she wants to see you and Mark. Why don't the two of you go in while I speak to Marcus about her care?"

Houston and Mark both nodded and went into the room. She was nervous as she got closer to a now awake Rachel. Now that she was awake, Houston couldn't find any words. She had prepared herself for Rachel passing and never thought about being able to talk to her again.

"I heard your voice," Rachel said on a whisper.

"You heard my voice?" Houston said.

"Yes I did. I heard you call me Mommy."

Tears rolled down Rachel's face and Mark moved to wipe them away.

"Don't cry Mom," he said.

"Mark, my prayers have been answered. Houston is here. You're here and I'm still here to embrace you both," she said.

Houston and Mark moved at the same time and leaned over on two different sides of the bed and hugged her. Rachel couldn't get up the strength to hug them back, but knowing that they were with her and hugging her was enough for her.

"I am so sorry Houston."

"Mommy, please don't apologize. I know that it's been thirty years of hurt, but that's thirty years in the past and today is a new day. Today I have you, I have Mark and you have us both and we love you. That's all that matters."

"You're right and I love you both. I'm glad you have each other now. Deep down I knew God would work this out. I didn't know how, but I had faith."

"Mom, what do you remember? The doctor told us you didn't remember the accident."

"Well, I remember heading to the airport to catch a flight to Florida because I was going to try and talk to Houston's dad. I remember I was heading toward the interstate and that's it before Houston started talking to me each day about her life for the past thirty days."

Rachel's comment rocked Houston to her core.

"Wait, you remember me talking to you all this time?"

"Yes I do. I heard you talking about everything from your first birthday party with the frilly pink and white dress on, all the way through meeting a wonderful man and postponing your wedding to come here to be with me. I heard every word you said, but I couldn't figure out how to talk back to you to let you know I could hear you. I also heard you call me Mommy earlier today and when I felt myself slipping away, I felt a push from God and I heard him say, 'Not yet Rachel'. The next thing I remember is hearing the beeping of the machine and hearing each of your voices. I couldn't make out who was who, but I could hear them."

"Well, I'm here, Mark and of course Marcus. Ms. Lana is also here along with my dad and Noah, my fiancé."

Rachel looked square at Houston with wide eyes.

"Did you say your dad was here?" she asked.

"Yes. He and Noah flew out today to be with me because we didn't know what to expect when they cut the machines off and they wanted to be here for support. I'm sorry you were in an accident, but I'm glad to hear you were coming to see me. Marcus also gave me your box, the one with my name on it with the letters to me you've written over the years. A lot of the questions over the years that I had about you were answered and now it looks like we'll have at least another thirty years to share our lives."

"You've read my letters?"

"Well, not all of them, but I read through most starting from the beginning and then I skipped to the last one where I was able to read that you were coming to Florida and were hoping to mend fences."

"Yes I was," Rachel smiled. "I had already waited too long to make that first step and no matter how we got to this first step, we're here and I'm never looking back, but pressing forward. Thank you for being here and thank you for your daily letters to me. I heard every word and I am happy that you had a very happy life and I never had a doubt that leaving you with your father was the right decision. He and Anna did a great job."

"Yes they did and we're all thankful that you gave me life."

Rachel then turned to Mark.

"When did you get here? I'm so happy to see you. I've really missed you."

"I've missed you too, Mom and I got in today. It took a while to get me from the naval cruiser I was on after Dad was able to get word to the military who were finally able to reach me about a week ago."

"So what do you think about having a big sister now?" Rachel asked.

"I think I'm going to like it. I may hit her up for a few dollars since that's what big sisters are supposed to do and I've never been able to do that," he laughed.

They all laughed and hugged again and this time Rachel was able to lift her arms a little to grab on to both kids lightly.

"We are going to step out to let Marcus come in and then let you get some rest and I promise we'll be here when you wake up later. I'm not going anywhere," Houston said, meaning every word.

"Okay. I am very tired, but I want to see Marcus before I fall asleep. You two stay close because I'm going to want to see you both when I wake up. I'd like to speak to your dad as well."

"I'll go get them," Houston stepping out to give Mark a few moments alone with Rachel.

Chapter 36

Houston felt like she could walk on clouds she was so happy. Rachel had been steadily getting better each day and after a few more days in intensive care so that they could monitor her closely, she'd spent the last week in a regular room. The doctors have given her the okay to be released and in a few hours they would be welcoming her home to finish her recovery.

Houston was both happy and sad because a few days after Rachel settles in at home, she would have to return to her life in Florida. The date of her wedding which had been postponed was coming up in a few weeks and she had lots to do.

Her father and Noah had already returned to Florida. She was happy to hear that her father and Rachel were able to talk and came to an understanding that what mattered most to them both was Houston's happiness. They decided to not rehash what happened thirty years ago, finding no purpose in doing so. They were moving on from that and were looking ahead at becoming a blended family and sharing their love for her.

She, Mark and Ms. Sophia were almost done with the decorations and as she watched the time, she knew that Marcus would be home any minute with Rachel. They were planning a small family celebration and when Rachel was up to it, they would have a bigger celebration that included other family and close friends.

After the decorations were complete and Houston was able to shower and change her clothes, she sat down while she applied her make-up and thought about how drastically her life had changed. Nothing could have prepared her for being able to spend time with Rachel, getting to know her and sharing each other's lives. A trip that she thought would turn into a sad one turned out to be some of the best times of her life.

She continued to go to the hospital every day to spend time with Rachel, who loved that Houston now called her Mommy all the time. She called Anna Mom so each had their own name and title with the same kind of love from and for her. They were even making plans for Rachel to fly to Florida for the wedding as long as she was given the okay to fly by her doctor. Looking ahead, the doctor stated he saw no reason she wouldn't be able to fly by then so excitement was in the air that her special day would now include Rachel, her step-father and her brother.

Houston stood in the door as she watched Marcus help Rachel exit the car. In her mind, she was that one year old baby and she was watching her mother come home to her. This, she thought was well worth the wait.

SALUTES TO MOTHERS & GRANDMOTHERS

My Mom – Mrs. Lelia Elliott
By: JoAnn Wilson

I've seen you struggle; I've felt your pain,
I've seen you do it over and over again.

Get up when you're tired,
Put on clothes and go to work,
To take care of the family that you put first.

Working for less than you were worth,
Taking the hits, the abuse and worse.

But day after day, off to work you would go,
To clean someone else's house and mop their floors.

It's no wonder you came home tired and drained,
You gave it all you had so that we would gain,

I didn't understand it back then, but now it's all so
clear,
You did what you had to do – fierce, proud and without
a tear.

That's how I like to remember you, always trying to do
what is right,
In spite of what you had to go through, you did it with
all your might.

Raising two children with very little help,
Only God knows why you didn't cry, whimper or yelp.

And now in your senior years, I sacrifice for you,
Because of all you went through for me, it's the very
least I can do.

I want you to be comfortable and have everything you
need,
I want to bring a smile to your face every time you
think of me.

I want your latter to be greater than was your past,
I want you to know that you'll never have to ask.

For food or drink or anything else,
It's my turn to do for you what you wouldn't do for
yourself.

With fortitude, wisdom, love and grace,
You did what you could to run the race.

You never asked for much, God knows this is true,
But I want you to know, I'll do anything for you.

You lived your life for everyone else, and I'd love it if
now you would just think yourself,
But I know that isn't possible for you to do, so here I
am to make your wishes come true.

Thank you mom for your love and support,
Thank you mom that you never fell short.

Thank you mom for all you have done. But most
importantly, Thank you mom for a job well done.

I love you more than you'll ever know, so here are your flowers before you have to go.

If I haven't told you lately, I want to make it quite clear so that you know,
God's richest blessings on you I pray He will bestow.

I love you mom; that's the bottom line, I love you now and until the end of time!

Happy Mother's Day with all my love!!

JoAnn

My Mother, Like No Other
By: Cheryl Barton

Barbara Barton, There is None Like You

Can I get an AMEN for mothers! As I look back over my life and I reflect on the many ups and downs I've endured, I'm thankful that I've had a mother who never gave up on me.

I stand strong with my head held high, not caring about any obstacle that may come my way and try to block my blessed life. You've shown me through your endurance what it means to never give up and to never give in.

I've watched you sacrifice so that my brothers and I would have and you've loved us unconditionally. Not even a lifetime of gratitude would be enough appreciation for the life that I live because of who you are.

I could shout from every rooftop that I have the best mother in the world, but I don't have to because all you have to do is walk into a room and the love you have for us and for life is evident on your face, in your smile and in the way you speak about us.

All of the riches in the world couldn't take the place of having you love me and support me and for that, I'm am the richest person in the world. I am because you are and I love you.

My Mother, Like No Other
Written by: Cheryl Barton

Out here in this world, there is but one,
That one can't be compared because there is none.

She loves and cares and helps you with strife,
She does this in order to help you live a good life.

She doesn't ask for much and gives her all to you,
Nothing else measures up, her love is always true.

As she ages and her steps get slower,
Never leave her side, give back what you owe her.

She doesn't want your riches, your silver or gold,
She yearns for your presence, that's all? I'm sold.

She wears a badge, proudly displaying mother,
I'm glad to call her mother, my mother like no other.

Love, Cheryl

Tribute to Mother Dear
by: Mary J. Demory

This is dedicated to Mrs. Doris J. Smith "Mother Dear" as she was fondly called by her children and extended family. It seems like just yesterday that you were here with us, sitting in a chair in the kitchen; your favorite spot at your house, then Bernice's house and my house on weekends.

She was the matriarch of our family and her presence is deeply missed, yet her influence on our lives is still evident.

Mother Dear, you didn't have fortune or fame. You never strived for glamour or glitz, yet you touched so many with your quiet strength and love. You were a gentle giant. Without a doubt, you loved me unconditionally. You believed in me. You helped me to develop healthy self- esteem and to believe that I could achieve positive things in life in spite of our meager means. I was always "waiting for your ship to come in" to get some of the material things I wanted. Yet, as I grew older I realized that I had everything I really needed... YOUR LOVE.

The most important lesson you left with me was the one you lived by:

TRUST GOD, THE AWESOME RULER, THE GENTLE REDEEMER and lean not to my understanding.

Whenever there was trouble you would tell me that God spoke that into your spirit for me.

WHAT A LEGACY!

Mary J. Demory

To "Gommy" - My Grandmother
by: Chynae Barton

Dear Gommy,

You know that I love you so much and I'd do anything for you. I love all of the time that we spend together whether we're in the kitchen watching Judge Judy or Family Feud or riding around in the car with Daddy listening to gospel or Motown music.

You are the best grandmother to ever walk the face of this earth and the love and care that you have shown me all these years is something that is unmatched. You are so giving and so sweet, I've always witnessed you put the needs of others before your own and I've always tried to help you whenever I can.

When we have family gatherings, you always make sure everyone has everything they need and have enough food and I always make sure that you eat, too. Our weekly phone calls since I've started school always help me through any situation I may be going through. Just hearing your voice is always so soothing to me and when I talk to you, I feel like everything is going to be okay.

I know that you have always kept me covered in prayer and I know that there are certain situations that I couldn't have made it through without your guidance and the little pep talks that you give me every once in a while.

So many people look up to you and love you and that shows me that you are definitely walking in your purpose. The positive light that surrounds you is so bright and I always want to bask in it.

I love being around you even if we just sit in silence and say nothing and I cherish those moments. Everybody always calls, me, you, and Mommy triplets because we look so much alike and I love it.

I love when me, you, and Mommy have our girls day out on the weekends and we just ride around to different places and shop. Your house is a second home to me, it's always so warm and inviting and I have a lot of great memories in it.

Your relationship with Daddy is one that I hope I have the pleasure of experiencing when I get married one day. The love that you two have for each other is powerful and despite everything you two have been through, you always lean on each other for comfort and care.

You love your family unconditionally and that's something that a lot of people claim to do but don't really know how to, but you do it without a second thought.

I can never enter or leave your presence without getting a hug and kiss and that's something that I can always hold on to. I thank you for always being one of my biggest supporters in my journey through life and my search to find who I really am.

I love the relationship that you and mommy have. You two are close and do a lot together and talk every day and that's a great relationship to have and look up to. People always say that you can't pick your family, but if I could, I would choose this family time and time again. You have a loving spirit that drives and guides you in everything that you do and I love that about you.

You've been through so much, but never let anything keep you from smiling and enjoying life to the fullest. I don't know how you do it, but I hope you'll teach me one day. I love you very much and always will.

Love,
Chynae

A Letter to My Mother
Shirley Ann Melton
By: Adrienne Melton Better

Dear Mama,

I want you to know that along with Christ, you are the
center of my being—seriously. I can't wait for our
summer road trip.

Love always,
Ady

The Absolutely Perfect You

Before there was ever a Me, there was an Absolutely
Perfect You.
Always striving so hard to support me, to make my
dreams come true.

You brought me through life's lessons, with a
determine love when I had no clue.
You always provided for my every need, always
knowing just what to do.

The way you put us first before yourself, helped others
was something for me to aspire to.
I remember Gwynn Oak Park, Carlin's Drive-In
entertained us, but those were just a few.

I remember being spoiled at Christmas and birthdays,
and I still tell you what makes me blue.
I see you as the absolute best, open-hearted, hard
working as you repetitiously do.

Instilling faith, manners and kindness is a life-long
practice you gave that always gets me through.
You're the reflection of Christ, so perfect in every way, I
know this to be true.

So know on this forever, that no one could ever come
close in ever replacing you.
But most importantly know, YOU are deeply loved by
me, because you are the *Absolutely Perfect You*.

Love, Ady

*In Dedication to My Mother Who Was My Rock and
My Foundation
Cleo Davis*

By: Barbara White

Cleo Davis
January 10, 1922 – April 5, 2009

You can only have one mother, patient, kind and true,
No other friend in the entire world will be the same to
you.

When other friends forsake you,
To mother you will return,
For all her loving kindness,
She asks nothing in return

As I look upon her picture,
Sweet memories I recall,
Of a face so full of sunshine
And a smile for one and all.

Sweet Jesus, take this message,
To my dear mother up above,
Tell her how I miss her,
And give her all my love.

Barbara Y. White

The Style and Grace of My Grandmother
Mary E. Barton
By Cheryl Barton

Your name was Mary E. Barton and your game was style and grace. If I could share something about you that I know people admired it was your flare for your look and how you carried yourself. There were outfits with jewelry, handbags and shoes to match for every occasion.

Your house was the house where holidays were spent with lots of family fun, fellowship and of course food. So many of the recipes I now make for the family started in your kitchen. A lot of people take their history for granted, but I have always cherished the many lessons I learned from you and the many words of encouragement you often provided me with.

There is one story I love to tell that showed your love for God and how He was always protecting our family and I want to share it with the everyone.

One year when my daughter was a little over a year old, it had snowed really bad and the snow had turned to ice. Chynae was sleeping in the middle of the bed at your house and I reminded you that she was there, though she should have been in the crib. The roads were not drivable and we were snowed in for quite a few days and it was time to get more groceries. I had to walk to a local supermarket and before I left, I again reminded you that Chynae was sleeping on the bed and you were going to keep an eye on her and I knew you would.

When I returned, you were out front trying to move snow off of the steps and I asked where was Chynae. You said she was sleeping and I rushed up the stairs remembering she had been asleep on the bed. You told me you were sure she was still sleeping on the bed and when I opened the outside door, who was standing on the other side? None other than my one year old looking up at me grinning from ear to ear. I looked from her to the fifteen or so steps she had to come down to get to the front door, realizing she had never come down the steps on her own before. When I turned to tell you that she was no longer sleeping, but on the other side of the door I remember saying that she could have hurt herself or fallen down the stairs. Without missing a beat or a swipe of the broom, you said, God was watching out for her and she didn't fall or hurt herself because he carried her down the steps. You then told me to go inside and feed her now that she was awake because she was probably hungry.

I remember that day as if it had happened yesterday. I couldn't be upset and I love that now, my faith in God is strong because I watched your faith in Him carry you through every test and trial. I love and miss you daily!

Love Cheryl

Mommy, You are Special to Me
By Chynae Barton

Dear Mommy,

Let me start off by saying that you really are the best mommy in the entire world. You have always loved me and cared for me even when I did wrong. You never gave up on pushing me to follow my dreams and I will always appreciate that.

I'm always bragging about you to everyone I meet, telling them about all the new journeys you're taking in life and new ventures you come up with all the time that you want to take. You're the true definition of a go-getter and you really are every woman. Every time I hear that song, I think of you and how powerful you are and how strong of a woman you are. I can't think of a better role model to look up to than you and the fact that you're my mother makes it even better.

It's only been you and I for almost twenty-three years and we've been through ups and downs and everything we've been through has been a learning experience for the both of us. I've slowly, but surely grown and matured over these past few years with your help. You give me tough love and even though I tried to fight it for a long time, I now know that it's exactly what I needed and it helped shaped me into the young woman I am today.

As I get older, I'm noticing that I'm becoming more and more like you every day and people definitely have no problem pointing that out. If I'm out and see someone that knows you they always say I'm a "little Cheryl". Someone even told me they thought I was you from far away because I've developed your signature laugh.

I tried so hard to look in the wrong places for things to validate who I was when all I had to do was look to you and God. You've never known this, but when you used to go out at night to go line dancing or out with friends, I would stay up until you returned home just so that I knew you were safe. Every time I heard a garage door open or a car pass by, I would jump up to see if it was you and if it wasn't I would just get back in the bed and wait until you came home. When you would come in my room to check if I was sleep, I was pretending because I didn't know what I would say if you asked me why I was still awake.

Even if it was a time when we may not have seen eye to eye, I have always cared very much about you. I just never knew how to express it verbally until now. The ways that I knew how to express it were just by making you proud of me in things that I accomplished over the years.

You always tell me that parents love their children no matter what and if nobody has my back, you do. I look forward to the day when I walk across the stage at Morgan State University and receive my degree in Social Work and I know you'll be in the stands screaming your head off cheering me on. Being in college, has definitely been an eye opener for me. It's made me appreciate you and everything that you have done for me.

I have met people who have never had a relationship with their mother or had to deal with the loss of their mother and it made me think about what I would ever do if I lost you. The truth is that thought is too painful for me to even think about. Even when we have disagreements, there's no one that I would rather have as a mother than you and I don't know how I would survive if I didn't have you in my life. You've always wanted what was best for me and I want what's best for you as well. You have a powerful voice that needs to be heard by the world, and I know that you plan on making that happen.

You are incredibly talented and skillful in too many things to count. Almost every time that I talk to you, you've discovered yet another thing you want to pursue to become skilled in or you've finished another book and are working on a new one all while still working a full time job. That's highly admirable and I strive to be that ambitious and goal-oriented every day.

As a single mom, you definitely broke all the barriers and went above and beyond the call of duty to take care of me as well as yourself. At times, it may have been difficult, but you put on a brave face and prayed your way through and God has and is continuing to bless you because of it. I've watched you go through numerous losses in the family, and with each one you were always the one being strong for everyone else and even as a child, I always felt that it was my job to protect you. I saw you taking control of every situation, but I know there are times when you just want to have a quiet day to yourself with no interruption and nobody asking you for anything.

When I'm on campus at school or out with friends, I love sending you a text letting you know I'm thinking about you and making sure you're still here with me. Even if you send back a simple "ok" I'm satisfied because at least I know that you're still here.

I love those days when you vent to me about things that happened at work or in other areas of your life because I know that means that you trust me and that's what I've always wanted. I often find myself reflecting on the things we went through as mother and daughter over the years, and though a lot of those events could have been avoided, they forced me to look at myself in a new light. I knew that there were changes I needed to make to better myself as well as help our relationship grow. I know that there's a reason for everything that you tell me whether I want to hear it or not and even when it seems like I may not be listening or paying attention, I am.

I remember every piece of advice you've given me regarding certain topics and when I have children of my own one day, I hope that I can be as good of a mother to them as you have been to me. I know that they will be spoiled rotten by you because I was, even though I hate admitting it. I've never wanted for anything and I have you to thank for that.

When I decide to get married one day, I'll take into consideration all of the things you said that a good husband should do for his wife. Like I said, I'm always paying attention to everything you say.

I love how our relationship continues to grow as mother and daughter and because of God, it's where it's supposed to be.

I look forward to all the time we will spend together in the future and all the trips we'll take together, all the talks we'll have and especially all the line dances you'll teach me. All of these moments are ones that I cherish and they mean more to me than any material thing ever could. I love you forever and ever.

With Love,
Chynae

Also Available from Barton Publishing, LLC:

One Sister Away: Encouraging Words From One Sister to Another, Volume 1

A Purpose-Filled Dash: Living an Empire State of Mind

Coming Soon from Barton Publishing, LLC:

One Sister Away: Encouraging Words From One Sister to Another, Volume 2

About Barton Publishing, LLC

Barton Publishing, LLC is a company dedicated to helping writers become authors. Our foundation is based on the belief that there is a writer in all of us just waiting to be birthed. Get moving toward that dream today!

Our company motto is, "Your Dreams Are Safe in Our Hands" and we stand behind that.

For more information on the services provided by Barton Publishing, visit our website at
www.bartonpublishingLLC.com

www.ingramcontent.com/pod-product-compliance
Lightning Source LLC
Chambersburg PA
CBHW051829040426
42447CB00006B/446